# HOW THE BIBLE CAN HELP US UNDERSTAND

---

# APPROACHING THE END OF LIFE

# HOW THE BIBLE CAN HELP US UNDERSTAND

# APPROACHING THE END OF LIFE

*A Bible study for individuals or groups*

# VIRGINIA MOFFATT

DARTON·LONGMAN+TODD

First published in 2020 by
Darton, Longman and Todd
1 Spencer Court
140 – 142 Wandsworth High Street
London SW18 4JJ

Copyright © 2020 Virginia Moffatt

ISBN: 978-0-232-53427-6

A catalogue record for this book is available
from the British Library

Designed and produced by Judy Linard

# CONTENTS

| | | |
|---|---|---|
| SERIES INTRODUCTION | | 7 |
| INTRODUCTION | | 11 |
| 1 | THE INEVITABILITY OF DEATH | 15 |
| 2 | PREPARING FOR DEATH | 32 |
| 3 | THE ACT OF DYING | 52 |
| 4 | CONTROLLING THE END OF LIFE | 71 |
| 5 | LIFE AFTER DEATH | 97 |
| CONCLUSION | | 121 |
| ACKNOWLEDGEMENTS | | 127 |

# SERIES INTRODUCTION

The Bible is the collection of writings and prayers pulled together by people and prophets over a period spanning approximately fifteen centuries[1] to describe humanity's relationship with God. It has great value for the three monotheistic religions, Judaism, Christianity and Islam, but as the key text of Christianity it plays a particularly vital role in the lives of Christians. Originally communicated orally, the written words of the Bible reflect the history, culture and theological understanding of the times in which they were written. In some instances, this can lead to contradictions, confusion and disagreements about its meaning. Nonetheless, the search for answers and collective wisdom found in the Bible's pages continue to make it highly relevant for the world we live in today.

The Jerusalem Bible was first published in 1956 by French scholars at the École Biblique in Jerusalem, in response to Pope Pius XII's encyclical suggesting a translation from Greek and Hebrew texts. In 1966, Darton, Longman and Todd published an English version of the Jerusalem Bible, using the French text as the basis. This version was edited by Alexander Jones and included contributions from well-known Catholics such as J R R Tolkien, and has always been praised for its literary qualities. Nineteen years later the New Jerusalem Bible edited by Dom Henry Wansbrough was published. Translated directly from the Greek and Hebrew, it incorporated new scholarship, fresh study material and the experience of two decades of use in churches. In 2019, Darton, Longman and Todd published the Revised New Jerusalem Bible, also translated by Dom Henry. This significantly changed version comes complete with updated study notes and inclusive language. It is the first new translation of the Bible in the twenty first century and has already been widely praised.

To celebrate the launch of the Revised New Jerusalem Bible, Darton, Longman Todd have commissioned this series of study guides to the Bible. Recognising how much the Bible can teach us today and using the RNJB as the translation for the text, each book will take an aspect of life and ask how the Bible can help us understand it better. Each book will be written by a Catholic who will bring their own perspective to the subject matter. The authors are drawn from lay and religious, people with theological training and those without. Where many Bible Study Guides are written by Bible experts, this series is taking a different approach. Each author has been commissioned to write from their unique lived experience, using their personal response to key Bible passages to throw a light on the topic under discussion, reinforcing the intent of the

Revised New Jerusalem Bible to be a Bible for 'study and proclamation'.

## HOW TO USE THESE STUDY GUIDES

The format of these study guides is very simple. There will be a brief introduction to the topic, followed by 5 or 6 chapters picking up a key theme, leading to a concluding chapter. Each book is short enough to read in one sitting so you may find benefit from reading it through once before you start using it for study, and then focussing on one chapter at a time. You may wish to take notes as you go, to help with your reflections. Each book is designed to be read either privately or as part of a small study group.

1. Read the chapter through to gain an understanding of the author's arguments. Have a think about what they are saying, do you agree, do you disagree? Have you seen something in a different light?
2. Re-read again, focussing on the Bible passages referred to. Are the texts familiar to you? What do you think of the author's interpretation? Do you have an alternative one? Is this helpful to your life?
3. Each chapter is broken into sections with questions for you to reflect on. Use them as a springboard for further thought and your own independent study of the Bible.
4. The author's ideas and interpretations on the biblical texts cited are their own. Readers may not agree with every position

taken, but it is hoped that these guides will help provoke thought and deepen your own understanding of the issues.
5. Follow the recommended actions and review afterwards whether it has helped or hindered your understanding.
6. Use the final prayer and the Bible texts referred to in the chapter to pray about the issues highlighted.
7. If undertaking this guide as a group, please do consider how you might ensure you are accessible to everyone. This could include welcoming housebound people to participate via Skype, inviting people from every community in the parish, and ensuring it is at a time to suit parents and carers.

The study guides are produced in pairs with overlapping themes. This study guide on the end of life is published alongside Frank Cottrell-Boyce's book on forgiveness, something that will be touched on later. Though each book has been written as a standalone reflection, some readers may find merit in studying both.

Virginia Moffatt
Series Editor

**NOTES**
1. *When was the Bible Written?*, International Bible Society Website: https://www.biblica.com/resources/bible-faqs/when-was-the-bible-written/
2. Frank Cottrell-Boyce, *How the Bible Can Help Us Understand Forgiveness* (Darton, Longman and Todd, 2020).

# INTRODUCTION

Life is rarely full of certainty, but there is one thing we can all be sure of. One day, though we can't know exactly which day, every one of us will die. While this may be one of the oldest clichés in the book, it is still the truest thing we know. And that knowledge can be terrifying, liberating or both. We are fortunate, as Christians, to have the Bible to turn to, as a guide in our journey through life, particularly because it provides us with a constant reminder that 'in the midst of life, we are in death'. God created the world in which we live, as a world of impermanence, in which everything comes to an end eventually. Gerard Manley Hopkins' famous poem 'Spring and Fall' captures this sense perfectly:

> Márgarét, áre you gríeving
> Over Goldengrove unleaving?
> Leáves like the things of man, you
> With your fresh thoughts care for, can you?
> Ah! ás the heart grows older
> It will come to such sights colder
> By and by, nor spare a sigh
> Though worlds of wanwood leafmeal lie;
> And yet you wíll weep and know why.
> Now no matter, child, the name:

> Sórrow's spríngs áre the same.
> Nor mouth had, no nor mind, expressed
> What heart heard of, ghost guessed:
> It ís the blight man was born for,
> It is Margaret you mourn for.

Like the poet, the writers of the Bible are long dead, but like him, they also sought universal truths about life and death; as a result the Bible is full of helpful insights on what it means to live and die. This study guide provides an opportunity to consider what we can learn from such reflections, which hopefully will help us increase our understanding of approaching the end of life.

As I have been writing this book, I have taken time to think about my own views on life and death and seeking out the views of others particularly those who have accompanied the dying, either as ministers, health care professionals or in a voluntary capacity. I have also sought out scriptural passages that I feel shed light on a particular aspect of the subject, not as a theologian (because I have no formal training in theology) but as a lay Catholic trying to learn from the Bible and share my personal insights. Any mistakes I may have made in interpretation are mine, but I hope that readers of this study guide will use these passages a springboard for your own explorations into how you think about death.

The format of this book is quite simple. In Chapter 1 I explore the inevitability of death and why it frightens us. In Chapter 2, I take a look at how we might prepare for death – our own and the deaths of people we know and love. How do we envisage our own deaths? How can we help a friend or family member who is dying? Chapter 3 will consider what makes a good death, and how we can support people in their final moments. Modern times and the advance of medicine have thrown up many ethical questions about when how to manage the end of life. The fourth chapter will examine these issues, and ask if the Bible can help us reach any conclusions. In Chapter 5, I will consider how the rituals of mourning can focus our attention in the wake of an immediate bereavement, and how Bible passages can comfort in our time of grief. Such grief can be devastating, and I will reflect how we can find a way to continue living when someone we loved has died.

I'm acutely aware that talking about death and dying can bring up painful issues and each chapter might trigger memories that are hard for group members. I recommend that group leaders discuss with members first if there are any particular areas that may be difficult and that each session is conducted with sensitivity allowing for participants to take a break if the subject matter is overwhelming at any point.

# 1
# THE INEVITABILITY OF DEATH

**'All humanity is grass,
and all its beauty like the wild flower.
The grass withers, the flower fades.'**
***Isaiah 40:6***

I vividly remember the first time I really thought about death. It was a bright sunny day when I was about 9 or 10. I was at school in the queue to go back in after lunch break, standing about half way up the steps, when I suddenly found myself thinking about a prayer: 'Glory be to the Father, to the Son and the Holy Spirit. As it was in the beginning, is now and ever shall be world without end. Amen.'

I had been saying that prayer all my life, but for some reason, that day, I stopped to think about its meaning. 'World without end' was heaven, I assumed, the place I had been told I would go when I died. I had experienced death by then: that of my Auntie Winifred (when I was about 5), and of my grandmother (when I was nearly 8). Both had died at our house, nursed by my mother, and though I had been too young to make sense of the experiences, both deaths stayed with me. As well as that, my best friend's mother ran a nursing home so I was used to going round to play there and hearing about the death of a resident to whom I might have spoken a few weeks before.

I didn't really think about these deaths that day in the queue at school. I just had a sudden realisation that one day my life would end, and eternity would follow. The thought terrified me. I don't remember talking to anyone about it, though if I mentioned it to my mother she'd have probably been reassuring about the fact death was a long way away, and I had my whole life ahead of me. But from the moment I had that thought, I couldn't ever forget that at some point I, and everyone I love, everyone I know, everyone in the world, will eventually die.

I am 54 now, nearer to my end than my beginning. I've experienced a lot more deaths since then, some close, some not so close. I am grateful to have grown up in the Catholic faith which has from the very first, made clear the inevitability of death, and given me a framework in which to try and understand it. The Bible is part of that framework. From the Wisdom Books which explore the meaning of life, death and suffering, to the New Testament revelations that Jesus died and rose for us, there are plenty of places where we can seek answers to our questions and find guidance and understanding.

The fear of death that I first experienced as a child is probably a universal emotion, and one, I think, that has several elements.

# 1  THE FEAR OF NOT MATTERING

> Vanity of vanities, says Qoheleth, vanity
>     of vanities. All is vanity!
> What profit is there for anyone in all
>     that toil, toiling under the sun?
> A generation goes, a generation comes,
>     yet the earth stands firm for ever.
> The sun rises, the sun sets; then to its
>     place it speeds and there it rises.
> Southward goes the wind, then turns
>     round to the north;
> round and round it goes;
> then back on its circles goes the wind.
> Into the sea go all the rivers, and yet the
>     sea is never filled;
> to the place where the rivers go
> there they continue to go.
> All things are wearisome, more than
>     anyone could express.
> The eye does not have enough of seeing,
> nor the ear its fill of hearing.
> What was, will be again,
> what has been done, will be done again,
> and there is nothing new under the sun!
> There is something of which it is said,
> 'Look here! This is new!'
> It existed in the ages before us.
> There is no memory of the past
> nor will there be among those who
>     come
>
> *Ecclesiastes 2:1-11*

The book of Ecclesiastes was written sometime between 450 and 200 BC and has been ascribed to 'Qoheleth'. The author self identifies with Solomon, the father of Wisdom in Israel, but his real identity is unknown. The name 'Qoheleth' simply means 'person of the assembly' and the writer may have been a leader or preacher, who chose to create this literary fiction in order to place his work firmly in the Wisdom tradition. It probably doesn't matter, as the book of Ecclesiastes speaks a universal truth to us.[1] The passage above is a prime example as it sets out the key themes of the book – the futility of human existence, the immutability of the world, the sense that nothing we do ever amounts to much. It is a familiar lament that strikes a chord in every human heart. We like to think that we matter: what we do, say, how we act. After all we are heroes in our own story. Life revolves around us, doesn't it? So what happens to us when we walk off the page? Where do we go? And what will we leave behind us? Will anyone remember us for very long? What we did, what we failed to do? Who we hated, who we loved? Do our lives have any real meaning if the moment they have ended they are not remembered?

Qoheleth's fear resonates with us because once two or three generations have passed, there will be no-one left on earth who will have known us while we were alive. The book of Ecclesiastes wrestles with this conundrum. We can live a happy life, achieve status, wealth and riches, but in the end it all fades away. Qoheleth's solution is to recognise that God has gifted us with life and understanding of our situation and that by trusting in God, who lasts for ever, or lives will have meaning:

> What do people gain from the efforts they make? I have seen the task that God has given people to labour at. All that he does is apt for its time; but although he has given human beings an awareness of the passage of time, they can grasp neither the beginning nor the end of what God has done. I know there is no happiness for a human being except in pleasure and enjoyment through life. And when we eat and drink and find happiness in all our achievements, this is a gift from God. I know that whatever God does will be for ever.
>
> *Ecclesiastes 3:9-14*

## *Questions for reflection*
- Do you ever think about death? Is it something that scares you?
- What do you think about the first passage from Ecclesiastes? Does life ever seem vain to you?
- Do you agree with Qoheleth that trusting in God gives life meaning?

## 2  THE FEAR OF SUFFERING

*Song Psalm. Of the sons of Korah. In sickness, In suffering. Poem for Heman the native born.*

O Lord and God of my salvation,
I cry before you day and night.
Let my prayer come into your presence.
Incline your ear to my cry.
For my soul is filled with evils;
my life is on the brink of Sheol.

I am reckoned as one in the tomb;
I am like a warrior devoid of all strength,
like one roaming among the dead,
like the slain lying in their graves,
like those you remember no more,
cut off, as they are, from your hand.

You have laid me in the depths of the pit,
in regions that are dark and deep.
Your wrath weighs down upon me;
I am drowned beneath your waves.
You have taken away my friends;
to them you have made me hateful.

Imprisoned, I cannot escape;
my eyes are sunken with grief.
I call to you, Lord, all day long;
to you I stretch out my hands.

# The Inevitability of Death

Will you work your wonders for the dead?
Will the shades rise up to praise you?
Will your mercy be told in the grave,
or your faithfulness in the place of perdition?
Will your wonders be known in the dark,
your righteous help in the land of oblivion?

But I, O LORD, cry out to you;
in the morning my prayer comes before you.
Why do you reject me, O LORD?
Why do you hide your face from me?

I am wretched, close to death from my youth.
I have borne your trials; I am numb.
Your fury has swept down upon me;
your terrors have utterly destroyed me.

They surround me all the day like a flood;
together they close in against me.
Friend and neighbour you have taken away:
my one companion is darkness.

*Psalm 88*

Psalm 88 speaks to another major fear about death – the fear that it will bring pain and suffering. We cannot know the time and manner of our death until it comes upon us. But, unless we die in our sleep, we know we are likely to experience some pain before the end, either through sickness or severe injury. Nobody in their right mind would wish to endure pain and yet it is the nature of human existence that we do and that in our final hours, or even years, we may experience it frequently. And the Psalmist speaks of a deeper fear that in the worst of our suffering our friends will turn away, repulsed by our sickness; that we will be left alone and even God will abandon us in the dark.

We find countless examples of faithful people struggling with pain in the Bible. Psalm 22 begins in despair: *'My God, my God, why have you forsaken me?'* later describing how, *'Like water I am poured out/disjointed are all my bones.'* The psalmist of Psalm 41 describes how people who hate him feel he deserves the sickness he is suffering, saying that, *'Something deadly has fastened upon him;/he will not rise from where he lies'*. The whole of Job recounts the prophet's suffering as he becomes sick and is abandoned by all who surround him. And of course, this culminates in the suffering that Jesus endures on the cross, where at his darkest moment, he cites Psalm 22 asking why God has forsaken him.

And yet, for every cry of despair, there is also faith that God will not ignore suffering, but instead will accompany the sufferer. Psalm 42 concludes with the hope that: *In my integrity you have upheld me/and have set me in your presence for ever*. Psalm 22 may begin in desperation, but it ends with the psalmist praising the Lord who *'has not hidden his face,/but he listens to the cry of the poor.'* At the end of the book of Job the prophet is restored to health, while all four Gospel writers show that Jesus is released from his pain early, rather than dying an agonisingly prolonged . In Mark's version, Pilate is 'astonished' (Mark 15:44) that this has happened, while in John's the Roman soldiers arrive to break his legs (to speed on death) only to discover Jesus is already dead (John 19:33-34). Thus the Bible writers show us that while it is likely we will endure such suffering at the end of our lives, we can also rely on God to come to our aid and comfort us in our pain, as the book of Ecclesiasticus notes:

> He sees and recognises how wretched their end is
> and so he makes his forgiveness the greater.
> The compassion of human beings extends to neighbours
> but the Lord's compassion extends to everyone.
> 
> *Ecclesiasticus 18:12-13*

## Questions for reflection
- Do you ever fear that your death might be painful?
- What do you think would help you deal with it?
- What will you want from God when you are dying?

## 3 THE FEAR OF THE UNKNOWN

> To this there is nothing to add,
> From this there is nothing to subtract –
> and the way of God inspires awe.
> What is, has been already,
> What will be, is already;
> God seeks out what has gone by.
>
> Again I have seen under the sun:
> crime is where justice should be,
> the criminal is where the righteous
>     should be.
>
> And I thought in my heart, the righteous and the criminal will both be judged by God, since there is a time for every thing and every action here. I thought in my heart on the subject of human beings: this is so that God can test them and show them that they are animals. For the fate of a human and the fate of an animal is the same: as the one dies, so the other dies; both have the same

> breath. Human is no way better off than animal, for all is vanity.
>
> Everything goes to the same place, everything comes from the dust, everything returns to the dust.
>
> Who knows if the human spirit mounts upward or if the animal spirit goes downward to the earth? I saw there is no contentment for a human being except to rejoice in works. Such is their lot: no one can tell what will happen after they are gone.
>
> *Ecclesiastes 3:14-22*

Although Qoheleth suggests that faith in God gives us purpose, and that God is there before, after and beyond us, he still cannot be sure what happens to us. Again, this is a very universal fear. Just as we cannot imagine our existence before our birth, it is very difficult to imagine what happens after we are gone. And the thought of what comes next can be terrifying.

So does the Bible have any indication of what happens after we die? Many Old Testament writers believed in life after death, suggesting that living well would unite us with God. But while it is made clear to us that this heaven is better than earth, it is unclear what such a life will look like. Is it a place of the spirit as referred to in Ecclesiastes 12:7: *'the dust returns to the earth from which it came, and the spirit returns to God who gave it.'*? Or is it perhaps a physical place, where we are reborn into newer, better bodies, as Isaiah seems to suggest:

> On this mountain the Lord Sabaoth is
>     preparing for all peoples
> a banquet of rich food, a banquet of
>     fine wines,
> of succulent food, of well-strained wines.
> On this mountain, he has destroyed
> the veil which veiled all peoples,
> the pall enveloping all nations.
> He has destroyed death for ever.
> Lord God has wiped away the tears
>     from every cheek;
> He has taken his people's shame away
>     over all the earth,
> for the Lord has spoken.
> And on that day it will be said,
> 'Look, this is our God,
> in him we put our hope that he would
>     save us.
> This is the Lord, we waited for him.'
> *Isaiah 25:6-9*

Jesus also talks about heaven frequently in the New Testament, though he speaks so often in parables, it can be hard to pin down exactly what heaven is. The kingdom of heaven is compared to a mustard seed, a hidden treasure, a precious pearl and a banquet, and it is frequently suggested that it is a place where people are valued, loved, treated equally. Jesus often says that the kingdom of heaven is at hand, which early Christians interpreted as meaning that the end of the world was imminent. However, once it became clear that this wasn't the case, Christians have had to come up with other explanations. Today many Christians conclude that our job is to build the kingdom of heaven in the here and now, and work to create a world where all people are treated with justice and compassion.

While this is a valid explanation of how we might live on earth, it still doesn't get us closer to understanding what life is like after we die. As Jesus' death approaches, he talks about going to sit at the right-hand side of his father, though this isn't fully described. The gospels of Luke and Mark tell us Jesus ascended into heaven, but Matthew and John end with Jesus simply commissioning the disciples. As Christians we are taught to believe in life after death, the 'world without end' in the 'Glory Be' prayer that started me thinking about death. But what is this 'world without end'? What does it look like? What will it feel like? What does it mean to live for ever, and ever?

We believe Jesus rose from the dead and after the Resurrection appeared in his physical body. We believe that he 'ascended into heaven', where he sits at 'the right hand of the father'. But where is that, if it is not in the physical world? How will we get there after death? If our physical bodies have died here on earth, where will we go? How will we experience existence after that? We cannot possibly know, and that is why this fear of the unknown is so powerful.

Perhaps all we can do is fall back on the hope espoused in Hebrews 11:40 that *'God foresaw for us something better'*. We may not know what that something better looks like, but the life and death of Jesus gives us faith that if we follow his teachings, one day we will find out.

## *Questions for reflection*
- Do you believe in heaven and hell?
- If yes, what do you think they will be like? If no, what do you think happens after we die?
- Does belief in an afterlife make a difference to the way you approach death?

## TAKING IT FURTHER
As a group discuss your attitudes about death. Is this something you think about often? Do you talk about it with your family? Does this conversation make you want to discuss with family more?

You may also wish to attend a death café. Death cafes are the brainchild of Londoner Jon Underwood, who created them as an opportunity for people to come together and talk about death over tea and cake to help them think about the meaning of their lives.[2]

## CULTURE

**Dante's** *Divine Comedy*, a fourteenth-century Italian poem, written by Dante Alighieri, a year before his death. It is divided into three parts: Inferno, Purgatorio, Paradiso. Dante is accompanied, through hell, purgatory and eventually into Paradise by the poet Virgil. During his journey to God he encounters the evils of the circles of hell, encountering sins such as lust, avarice and anger. Moving through the mountains of purgatory, he discovers the seven roots of sinfulness. Having overcome these difficulties, he moves to the celestial sphere where he is faced with virtues such as fortitude and temperance, converses with saints and finally understands the nature of God's love for him.

*Everyman* is a late fifteenth-century English morality play that follows the fortunes of Everyman as he tries to encourage others to accompany him to heaven, dealing with issues of good and evil. Eventually Everyman learns he is alone on this journey and all he can bring to God is his good deeds.

*The Dream of Gerontius* is a poem by Cardinal John Henry Newman, put to music by Edward Elgar. It tells the story of the dying man as he comes to heaven. In Part 1 he is part hopeful, part fearful as he reaches the end of his life. He is joined by friends who pray with him and send him on his way. In Part 2, as a soul out of time and space, he is accompanied by his guardian angel past demons to meet God who judges him in a single moment. He is bathed in the lake of purgatory and reassured he will awake in glory.

*Gilead* by Marilynne Robinson is a modern novel about a priest, John Ames, in a small town in Iowa. John is dying and so writes a letter to the seven-year-old son he will never see grow up, reflecting on his life and the death he is facing.

*A Matter of Life and Death.* This seminal Powell and Pressburger film tells the story of Peter Carter a World War II RAF pilot who is shot down over the Channel. His miraculous survival turns out to be a mistake, and he must face a celestial court to argue that his life should continue.

**PRAYER**
### *A prayer to help with the fear of death*
Praise be You my Lord *through those who grant pardon for love of You and bear sickness and trial.*

Blessed are those who endure in peace, By You Most High, they will *be crowned.*

Praised be You, my Lord *through Sister Death,* from whom no-one living can escape. Woe to those who die in mortal sin! Blessed are they She finds doing Your Will.

No second death can do them harm. Praise

and bless my Lord *and give Him thanks,*
And serve Him with great humility.
> *Taken from the Canticle of Brother Sun and Sister Moon by St Francis of Assisi*

**NOTES**
1. Henry Wansbrough, *The New Jerusalem Bible Study Edition*, p. 1201 (London, Darton, Longman and Todd, 2018)
2. Death Cafe website, https://deathcafe.com/

# 2
# PREPARING FOR DEATH

**'For none of us lives for ourselves and none
of us dies for ourselves; for if we are alive,
we are alive for the Lord, and if we die,
we die for the Lord, and so, alive or dead,
we belong to the Lord.'**
***Romans 14:7-9***

Death is inevitable. It will happen to all of us whether we like it or not. And yet it is still something many of us are reluctant to talk about. A 2016 poll for Dying Matters found that although 64 per cent of people in the UK were happy talking about death with loved ones, 30 per cent were not and, after sex, death was the most uncomfortable subject for people to discuss.[1] While this is an improvement on previous years, that still means a third of people find death difficult to talk about. And having a faith doesn't seem to make a difference. A 2017 poll for Cooperative Funeral Care found that people of religious faith put off thinking about death longer than people of no faith, 27 per cent of Christians don't want to worry others by talking about it and 14 per cent are too busy living to talk about it.[2]

We clearly have a long way to go before talking about death comes easily to us, and yet if we are to prepare for our own death and others, we need to be able to have honest conversations about it. And perhaps we need to adjust the way we live. If, as Romans suggests we try to live our lives for God, it might be easier to then prepare to die in God. And the first step to doing that is to face up to our own mortality.

## 1 FACING OUR MORTALITY

> O Lord, you have been our refuge,
> from generation to generation.
> Before the mountains were born,
> or the earth or the world were brought
>     forth,
> you are God, from age to age.
>
> You turn people back to dust,
> and say, 'Return O children of Adam.'
> To your eyes a thousand years
> are like yesterday, come and gone,
> or like a watch in the night.
>
> You sweep them away like a dream,
> like grass which is fresh in the morning.
> In the morning it springs up fresh;
> by evening it withers and fades.
>
> Indeed, we are consumed by your anger;
> we are struck with terror at your wrath.

You have set our guilt before you,
our secrets in the light of your face.

All our days pass away in your wrath.
Our years are consumed like a sigh.
Seventy years is the span of our days,
or eighty if we are strong.
And most of these are toil and pain.
They pass swiftly and we are gone.

Who understands the power of your
  anger?
Your wrath matches our fear of you.
Then teach us to number our days,
that we may gain wisdom of heart.

Turn back, O LORD! How long?
Show pity to your servants.
At dawn, fill us with your merciful love;
we shall exult and rejoice all our days.
Give us joy for all the days of our
  affliction,
for the years when we looked upon evil.

Let your deed be seen by your servants,
and your glorious power by their
  children.
Let the favour of the Lord our God be
  upon us;
give success to the work of our hands.
O give success to the work of our hands.

*Psalm 90, 'On Human frailty'*

In some senses, Psalm 90, is somewhat bleak. Subtitled 'On human frailty' it really gets to the heart of the tenuousness of our existence. Although it begins praising God who is there for all ages, like some of Qoheleth's early passages in Ecclesiastes, the psalmist is full of regret for the transience of life. Humanity is returned to dust, while a 'thousand' years of humanity has passed like a 'watch in the night' for God. Our lives pass away like a 'sigh' and all we get is the seventy or eighty years allotted to us, many of them filled with pain. The psalmist suggests that God is angry with people and as a result we are fearful. Not a particularly encouraging relationship. And yet, the Psalm concludes with some optimism, if God can teach us 'to number our days' we can experience our lives more positively, we can 'exult and rejoice' and find 'joy' amidst our afflictions. In other words, if we can face up to the fact of our deaths, our lives will not only be fulfilling, but they will be truly authentic.

The 'span of our life is seventy years', used to be translated as 'three score years and ten' a phrase that was in common usage when I was younger. It was a phrase my father was very fond of; from an early age I can remember him saying that 'three score years and ten' was the age most of us would reach and that he would be happy to live that long. There were two implicit assumptions in this statement, firstly that death is inevitable and secondly that we have to make the most of the years we are given. My father achieved his aim, when he died in 1995, aged 71. And it only was after he died, that I realised his regular willingness to talk about life and death in this way, was helpful for me in preparing of his eventual death, and my own.

In fact, both my parents were very good at getting us to think about death. I went to my first funeral aged about three, and if the chief memory was eating ice cream and hiding under the table, I also remember arriving at the church, and people talking about the great aunt who was being buried. My childhood and teenage years were punctuated by many such funerals, while the constant regaling of family stories, reminded me that though people we loved had died, they were not forgotten. My mother loved graveyards, and if I was slightly freaked out by the holiday house situated next to one, as I grew older I learnt to appreciate her enthusiasm for them. She would often take us on detours on journeys home looking for some lost relative in a cemetery and even if we didn't discover the relative in question, we would usually find some interesting stories on the gravestones. So I learnt to love them too, particularly after surveying the flora of York's cemeteries as part of my dissertation project.

All of which was excellent preparation for thinking about my own mortality, and yet it is often very easy to brush such thoughts aside. When my husband tells me 'we are one day closer to the grave' I know he is right, but I don't like to dwell on it. I know my wonderful, frustrating, amazing, difficult, chaotic, joyful life will come to an end one day, but there's part of me that wishes it wouldn't. I may have stopped pulling out the grey hairs that are beginning to overwhelm the brown, but that doesn't mean I'm wholly reconciled to the fact I'm getting older and one day my life will be over. Or that I strive (and often fail) to live more healthily in the vain hope that this will also stave off the inevitable. Or that generally the minutiae of life gets in the way so I forget to think about my death because I'm to wrapped up in what we are having for dinner tonight. In his excellent book *Waiting for the Last Bus*[3] Richard Holloway, the former Bishop of Edinburgh, describes a pair of panels created by medieval artists in the chantry chapel in a church he knew as a young man. The panels depict a 'Dance of Death' – a skeleton who is dancing, while holding a carnation, next to a wealthy young man holding a purse. They are intended to remind worshippers that they are about to die, a 'memento mori', and that it is time they prepared for their deaths. As Holloway notes, in our increasingly health obsessed world it is important that we make sure we stop and reflect on such things. Accepting we are going to die doesn't need to be a negative, as noted above, it can help us live more fully because if we try to live like each day is our last, it can help remind us how precious and important life is, and we can live more joyfully as a result.

## Questions for reflection
- Do you find it easy to talk about death?
- How often do you think about your own death? Does it make you think differently about life?
- What are your thoughts about Psalm 90? Are there any other Bible passages that you have found helpful when thinking about death?

## 2 PREPARING FOR ANOTHER'S DEATH

> The LORD is my shepherd;
> there is nothing I shall want.
> Fresh and green are the pastures
> where he gives me repose,
> Near restful waters he leads me;
> he revives my soul.
>
> He guides me along the right path,
> for the sake of his name.
> Though I should walk in the valley of
>     the shadow of death,
> no evil would I fear, for you are with me.
> Your crook and your staff will give me
>     comfort.
>
> You have prepared a table before me
> in the sight of my foes.
> My head you have anointed with oil;
> my cup is overflowing.

> Surely goodness and mercy shall follow me
> all the days of my life.
> In the LORD's own house shall I dwell
> For the length of days unending.
> *Psalm 23*

When I asked friends on Facebook which readings were helpful to people who were dying, Psalm 23 was one of the most popular. It is not hard to see why. The Psalm is filled with beautiful imagery – the 'fresh and green pastures' and 'quiet waters' where the Lord will lead us feel safe, warm and comforting. The Lord 'revives my soul' and 'guides me along the right path'. The confidence the Psalmist has that God will be with us we walk 'in the valley of the shadow of death' is comforting. While the conclusion that we will live at the Lord's house 'for the length of days unending' is a hopeful one.

Knowing a friend or family member is dying, it can be hard to know how to respond. It is all too easy to not face up to the reality and avoid the subject, or to go in the other direction and bombard people with unhelpful opinions and advice. Wendy, a hospice nurse, suggests that what the dying person needs most from us is 'Understanding that this is the end of life. To be treated normally and honestly. Empathy not sympathy. Try and make memories together depending on time factor. Time not words.' Dr

Simon Woodman, a Baptist minister, says that people need to know their families and friends will be okay when they are gone, they need time to be with those they love and time to be alone. Catherine, a volunteer hospice worker, notes that people 'need sensitive, intuitive friends/family who can interpret their constantly shifting needs, but also competent, practical friends/family who can implement these things. Folk can fall into either category – seldom both. I think it is important for them to recognise and accept this, helping as they can, rather than worrying about what they cannot do for their loved one'. All three agree that managing pain is also critical, so having knowledge of options available, and a plan are essential.

Spending time with someone who is dying can be hard. It is tough seeing someone you love in pain and debilitated. I know I struggled a lot to deal with my mother's rapidly developing cancer, particularly when she was bed ridden and could hardly speak. She was a very gregarious person and loved to chat, so when speaking became difficult, I didn't always know how to be around her. Sitting by her bedside, I felt foolish talking to her, not sure if she could hear, and knowing she couldn't always respond. I wish I'd had the courage to speak more, as the day I did sit with her and read the prayers of the day, as I read the Psalm 'oh Lord let your hope rest in us as ours have rested in you' to my surprise she lifted her head, and joined in. And I realised that I had been remiss in not doing that before.

## Preparing for Death

Many dying people express regrets for mistakes they made, things they didn't do, friendships they lost. The most common regrets are not expressing feelings, too much time spent at work, not spending enough time with friends, allowing themselves to follow their dreams or be happier.[4] Hearing about such regrets is a salutary reminder of the point made earlier, that we have to live our lives as fully and as joyfully as we can, because once we reach the end, we will not be able to go back and fix it.

Preparing for a family member dying is even tougher when the relationship has broken down. We all fall out with people we love, and usually we find a way to say sorry, admit our fault, acknowledge hurts given and received, and reconcile. But we probably also all have had experiences where the problem became impossible to fix. Or felt like that. And time passes and before we know it, we haven't spoken in years. But sometimes it is possible to repair the damage before it is too late. When Margaret's father was dying, she found it a challenge to visit him. Her father had Asperger's Syndrome which meant throughout her life he had struggled to be warm and empathetic, making him a difficult person to love. Once he developed Alzheimer's a relationship with him became even more difficult, particularly when he forgot who she was: 'I thought it was too late to build any kind of relationship. My bitter-root expectation was that Dad would never change and it was too late to experience my heart's desire – to become a Daddy's girl.'

But Margaret persisted, and in the last days of her father's life, she turned her prayers from entreaties to make things better between them to thank God for the positive things, that he was dozing, that she could share information with the nurses to help him and so on. And then something amazing happened, as she was going over to his notes, he recognised her as his daughter, after two years of not knowing who she was. They spoke and he acknowledged he felt guilty, though he couldn't remember why. And suddenly she was able to tell him she forgave him everything and they were crying together. They parted on a joke,

> 'After I had gone through those doors, I felt overwhelmed and sat in the corridor, trying to make sense of what had just happened. It was so surreal! I had become a Daddy's girl. It's never too late for the Lord to bring healing!
>
> 'Dad still had dementia. He still had no idea where he was, or what season or year it was. It was as if he was living one side of a frosted window, and normal life continued the other side. Yet it seemed the finger of God had cleared a tiny hole, enabling Dad and I to communicate deeply through it. Everything else remained obscured, but … maybe it was the breath of the Spirit … I don't know… but it seemed a miracle – just for the two of us.'

## Preparing for Death

It takes courage and effort to do as Margaret did. Sometimes such courage and effort seem beyond us, or it is difficult to achieve even if we try. In my novel *The Wave*,[5] a group of people gather together on a beach knowing they cannot escape a tsunami. I wanted to explore what it means to face death in the book, and what it would be like for the characters, who had relationships that were broken. Three of my characters Poppy, Margaret and Yan have unreconciled conflicts with people they love. All three strive to put things right, knowing that they have very little time and they may have set themselves an impossible task. It would have been easy as a writer of stories to have neatly tied all their problems up in a bow, but I know life is more messy than this, and so instead, I tried to show good people with genuine grievances against each other, striving to understand, but struggling to forgive. And perhaps I wrote those characters as a reminder to myself and to all of us. Life is too short to fall out with people, too brief to hold grudges, we have to make room for forgiveness in our hearts.

### *Questions for Reflection*
- Have you ever accompanied a friend or family member through death? What was it like?
- What makes helping someone prepare for death easy? What makes it hard?
- Can the Bible be helpful when people are dying? Are there particular passages that you've found useful?

## 3 WHEN DEATH IS UNEXPECTED

> It was now about noon and darkness came over the whole land until mid-afternoon, as the sun's light failed. The curtain of the Temple was torn right down the middle. Jesus cried out in a loud voice saying 'Father, into your hands I commit my spirit.' Having said this, he breathed his last. When the centurion saw what had taken place, he gave glory to God and said, 'Truly this was a just man.' And when all the crowds who had gathered for the spectacle saw what had happened, they went home beating their breasts. All his friends stood at a distance, and also the women who followed with him from Galilee, watching these things.
>
> *Luke 23:44-49*

So far we've been thinking about preparing for death when someone is very ill or elderly and we know it is coming. But how do we deal with sudden death for which we are completely unprepared? The person who dies of a heart attack, or in a car accident, who takes their own life, or is killed in an act of violence? How can we prepare for something like that? The truth is we can't. And the impact can be devastating. Jesus's death is a good example of this. Although he had given plenty of warning of what was to come, his arrest, trial and subsequent execution is clearly shocking to his followers. When he dies, the sun fails, darkness falls, the veil of the Temple is torn. He cries out, and he is gone. The description works as pure narrative; this is, we believe, how the historic Jesus died. But it also works as a metaphor, for how else do we feel when someone dies unexpectedly but that a light has gone out, the temple is torn down? No wonder the people go home beating their breasts, the friends stand watching in a state of shock.

In a forthcoming memoir, *This Party's Dead*, Erica Buist writes movingly how she and her husband discovered his father's dead body, eight days after he had died. The shock of this caused her to become agoraphobic and obsess about her friends' health and wellbeing. As she slowly recovered, she realised that part of her problem was that she hadn't ever thought about death before. Researching the way other cultures deal with death, led her to conclude that she could learn a lot from them. So, over the last two years she has travelled round the world visiting death festivals where people are unafraid to speak of death and celebrate life at the same time.[6]

Simon Woodman says, 'A sudden death is very different from an 'expected' death – neither is 'easier' than the other, but the experience is dramatically different. I have heard it said, 'at least they didn't get old'. The phrase, 'God takes early those he loves the most' is often said, and in my experience is always unhelpful to relatives. Making sense of sudden death is very hard for people, and the funeral needs careful planning. One funeral service I took for a man who was killed in a car accident included the following: REM's song, 'Losing My Religion' (REM were a favourite band of his, and the choice was the family's); a prayer giving thanks for the life of the person, asking that good can come out of evil, asking for forgiveness for ways we may have hurt the person, committing the person to God's eternal loving embrace; Bryan Adams' 'Everything I Do'; symbolic action – people were invited to write memories of the person on cards and bring them to the front or hand them to the steward at the end to be passed to the family; I led a tribute summarising the person's life, and outlining the stages of grief, and reflecting the words of the family back to them; Gerry and the Pacemakers' 'You'll Never Walk Alone'.

The cruellest thing about sudden death is there is no time for the last-minute conversations, the appreciation of each other, the opportunity to resolve hurts. It can be so traumatic it can lead to extreme shock reactions like those experienced by Erica Buist, with the bereaved person needing a great deal of extra care.[7] And of course there are even more extreme versions that are even harder to deal with. When a family member has been murdered, for example, the bereaved are left with a deep trauma to add to the loss. This can be exacerbated by having to deal with the complexities of the criminal

## Preparing for Death

justice system and to have to listen to the horrors of the crime at inquests and trial.[8] I once had to attend part of a murder trial, and hear the evidence of what the murderers had done to the victim. The details were quite horrific and sickening to listen to. I cannot imagine how painful it must have been for the family. No wonder some people such as the families of the Moors Murders victims struggle to forgive the perpetrators.

Death by suicide is even more complicated. Suicide still has shameful connotations in our society, while some will blame the people closest to the person who died for what has happened, making it hard for the mourners to deal with the aftermath. Researchers estimate that at least six people will be profoundly affected by a suicide, and they are left with guilt for not seeing it coming, anger at being left behind and grief that the person they lost couldn't recognise how loved they were. It is important for the bereaved to be listened to, given space, and that the death is acknowledged. And for all to recognise that people who commit suicide are trying to put an end to their pain rather than their lives.[9]

Although death is always shocking, an unexpected death leaves us no chance to say goodbye to the person we loved. That's why planning the funeral carefully and finding creative ways to say goodbye, are so important. But in the end, all deaths are hard, all require us to offer and receive comfort and to remember God is with us in our grieving:

> he heals the broken-hearted;
> he binds up all their wounds.
>
> *Psalm 147:3*

## *Questions for reflection*
- In the passage from Luke, Jesus' friends watch his death at a distance, what do you think they were feeling?
- Have you ever had to deal with sudden death? Was it different from supporting someone with a long-term illness?
- Are there any Bible passages you feel particularly appropriate for dealing with sudden death?

## TAKING IT FURTHER
Write your own obituary. Try and be honest about your strengths and weaknesses. What do you think people will most miss about you? What do you think they'll remember? What would you like them to remember?

Talk to the group about the experience. How did it feel to think about how your death might be reported? Do you feel you have lived your life to the full to date? Or did it challenge you to do more?

## CULTURE
*The Big Chill.* In this 1983 film written by Lawrence Kasdan and Barbara Benedek and directed by Lawrence Kasdan, a group of friends

gather after the sudden death of their friend from university. As it emerges that his death was a suicide, they reflect on the impact of his loss and the changes in their lives since they were young.

***The End of Your Life Book Club*** by Will Schwalbe (Vintage Books, 2013). When the author's mother Mary Anne was dying of cancer, they began to swap books and an informal book club was born. A moving account of accompanying a dying relative and how books can bring comfort at such a time.

***The Quarry*** by Iain Banks (Little Brown and Company, 2014). In his final novel, Banks tells the story of Guy who is dying. As friends gather to say goodbye, his son Kit details his rage at his deteriorating condition and the humiliation of being cared for by his son.

***Waiting for the Last Bus: Reflections on Life and Death*** by Richard Holloway (Canongate, 2018). Richard Holloway, the former Bishop of Edinburgh, provides a series of reflections on life and death drawn from his experience of pastoral ministry.

***The Wave*** by Virginia Moffatt (Harper One More Chapter, 2019). A devastating tsunami is about to hit Cornwall. Realising they can't escape, a group of strangers gather on a beach to make their last hours count.

***This Party's Dead*** by Erica Buist (Unbound, forthcoming). When Erica Buist's father-in-law died, the shock of it made her agoraphobic. As she began to recover she decided to visit death festivals around the world, to explore how other cultures deal with death.

## PRAYER
### *A comforting prayer for the dying.*
> God,
> Help (insert name) discover your peace.
> Let them receive your comfort.
> Help them be at rest knowing you care
>     for them,
> And that you love them.
> Calm their soul as they move into the
>     afterlife.
> May they spend eternity with you;
> may they live forever in your presence.
> Amen.
>
> *Taken from the website Pray with me.*
> *https://www.praywithme.com/*

## NOTES
1. Com Res, *Dying Matters Coalition Public Opinion on Death and Dying*, April 2016 http://www.dyingmatters.org/sites/default/files/files/NCPC_Public%20polling%2016_Headline%20findings_1904.pdf
2. Co-op Funeral Care Media Report, *Making peace with death: National attitudes to death, dying and bereavement*, Cooperative Group Limited, 17 August 2018.

3. Richard Holloway, *Waiting for the Last Bus: Reflections on Death and Dying* (Edinburgh, Canongate, 2018).
4. Joe Martino, *The Top Five Regrets of the Dying* (Collective Evolution website 12/4/2013) https://www.collective-evolution.com/2013/04/27/the-top-5-regrets-of-the-dying/
5. Virginia Moffatt, *The Wave* (London, Harper One More Chapter, 2019)
6. Erica Buist, *This Party's Dead* (London, Unbound, Forthcoming)
7. Sudden Death website, *Sudden bereavement responses in the early weeks,* suddendeath.org: https://www.suddendeath.org/uncategorised/76-earlyweeks
8. Joan Dean, *Dealing with the death of a loved one is difficult, but a murder poses several problems*, The journal.ie 8 July 2017
   https://www.thejournal.ie/support-for-families-of-murder-victims-3482106-Jul2017/
9. Deborah Syani, *Understanding Survivors of Suicide Loss*, Psychology Today. 25 November 2013 https://www.psychologytoday.com/gb/blog/two-takes-depression/201311/understanding-survivors-suicide-loss

# 3
# THE ACT OF DYING

**'After Jesus had taken the wine he said, 'It is completed'; and bowing his head, he gave over his spirit.'**
***John 19:30***

The story of Jesus' arrest, trial, torture and death is central to all four Gospels. It is filled with painful moments. The agony in the Garden of Gethsemane when Jesus prays alone as his followers sleep, before accepting what is to come. The betrayal of Judas, and then of Peter. The trial, torture, and mocking of the soldiers. And the moments of kindness and compassion, Veronica wiping Jesus' face, the good thief asking for Jesus' prayers, and in John's version, Jesus has one last conversation with his mother and favourite disciple. Though crucifixion is a horrific and lingering death, Jesus dies quickly, recognising his life's work is at an end.

Jesus died violently and more painfully then most people, and yet his experience was utterly human. He was frightened like us, alone like us, at the mercy of other people who could be cruel or kind, like us. The fact that he was prepared for his end, helped him both endure the suffering and 'give up his spirit' when the time had come. It can teach us what we need to do to accompany those who die, to help them prepare, and to ensure their death is as pain free and positive as possible.

## 1 PREPARED FOR DEATH

> 'You may be sure of this, that if the householder had known at what time of the night the burglar would come, he would have stayed awake and would not have allowed anyone to break through the wall of his house. Therefore, you too must stand ready, because the Son of Man is coming at an hour you do not expect.'
>
> *Matthew 24:42-44*

The above passage was written at a time when early Christians believed the second coming was imminent. It would have been heard by its audiences as a message to warn people to be ready, to lead good lives, to work hard for the kingdom, so that when Jesus returned he would welcome them home. However, as the centuries have passed, and the end of the world hasn't occurred, it has taken on a different resonance, and one that is helpful to people who are dying. The message is to be prepared, to be ready for death, because as we saw in the previous chapter, we cannot know when it might happen. And if we are prepared, we are more likely to be able to accept it when it comes.

St Luigi Versiglia and St Callisto Caravario were Salesian priests working in China at the turn of the twentieth century. When they tried to protect three young girls from pirates, they were captured and beaten. As their captors took them away, they asked why the men had only begged for the safety of others, and not their own. Bishop Versiglia responded that they were priests and didn't fear death. He and Fr Callisto then heard each other's confessions. The other captors were released and then the two priests were shot.[1] In some versions of the story they were laughing as they died.

This is undoubtedly a story of great courage, and also a story that demonstrates how to make a good death. What made it possible for these two men to die this way and what can we learn from them?

Firstly, they were captured when they were in the middle of missionary work they believed in. They felt called to be with people in China, to minister to them and to bring God's word. Like many Salesians, Bishop Versiglia had opened a school and an orphanage, and once he was a Bishop he dedicated himself to his community travelling widely to meet parishioners across his Diocese. Fr Cavario too was committed to his work. Their ability to feel calm in the face of death, must in part, have been because they felt they were living their lives exactly as they should. Secondly, they had given each other confession, and so felt at peace with themselves, and able to leave the world without any regrets. And though they must have been anxious in their last hours, their deaths would have been mercifully quick, so they knew they might not be in too much pain. Finally, they were men of great faith, so for them, death was not the end, and would lead them to be united with God.

We cannot all be martyrs, and nor would we want to be (an excessive desire for suffering is an unhealthy impulse). However, we can certainly learn from their deaths. We can teach ourselves not to fear it (as mentioned in previous chapters) and when it comes we can look at it directly and acknowledge it is coming. Sometimes people in the public eye can help us with this. When Pope John Paul II was dying, he didn't flinch from showing us what dying looked like. He stood on the Vatican balcony giving his usual addresses, though his voice wavered, and his body shook. It was both painful to watch, because the man who we had seen as strong and vital, was clearly losing that bodily strength and his ability to speak. And yet, I also found it inspiring because he was saying, 'Look at me, look at my fading body, this is what happens to all of us in the end. Even so we can still live in hope, not in fear.' The *Big Brother* celebrity, Jade Goody, took a similar approach when she was diagnosed with cervical cancer, inviting the cameras in to film her last weeks. Not only did she do a great deal to raise awareness of the issue, but by showing her pains and joys to the world, it helped to demystify death. And it's an impact that has lasted – as I write, Channel 4 has just put out a documentary to mark a decade since she died. Not bad for someone who died aged 27.

Social media can also be a very powerful way to speak about death. In 2017, 95-year-old activist Harry Leslie Smith, fell ill and was rushed to hospital. Smith's son John had persuaded him to join Twitter several years previously and through his activism against austerity and on behalf of refugees he had become a huge public figure – 'the world's oldest rebel'. As he lay dying in a Toronto hospital his son took over his Twitter account, and for over a week people all around the world participated with John in his bedside vigil.[2] It was the most moving experience, to follow Harry from breath to breath until he took his last which proved inspiring to fellow activists around the world, giving John, the strength to continue his work.

## *Questions for reflection*
- What does the 'The Son of Man may come at an hour you don't expect' mean to you?
- Do you think it is possible to prepare for death? How would you do so?
- Have you been inspired by watching someone die? What did they teach you?

## 2  GOOD DEATH

> 'Do not be afraid for I have redeemed you:
> I have called you by your name, you are
>     mine.
> Should you pass through the waters,
> I shall be with you;
> through rivers, they will not swallow you up.
> Should you walk through the fire,
> you will not be scorched
> and the flame will not burn you.
> For I am the LORD your God,
> the Holy One of Israel, your Saviour.
> I have given Egypt for your ransom,
> Ethiopia and Seba in your stead;
> for you are precious in my sight,
> you are honoured and I love you.
> I therefore give people in your stead,
> and nations in return for your life.
> Do not be afraid for I am with you.
> From the east I shall bring your
>     descendants,
> From the west I shall gather you.
> To the north I shall say "Give them up!"
> to the south I shall say "Do not hold
>     them back!"
> Bring back my sons from afar,
> my daughters from the ends of the earth,
> all who bear my name,
> whom I created for my glory,
> whom I formed, whom I made.'
>
> *Isaiah 43:2-7*

At the hour of our deaths, we will want to be as pain-free as possible, to feel comforted and surrounded by love. The above passage, which we read as my mother was dying is one that I find immensely helpful. 'Do not be afraid' says the Lord, for 'I have called you by your name'. However painful things get, God is with us, the waters will not swallow us up, the fire will not scorch us. We are known, loved, 'precious' in God's sight. And the Lord will bring our descendants, our sons and daughters to be with us.

My mother had a good death. She was diagnosed with secondary breast cancer in February 2014 and died that May. She had always been healthy and fit, so the diagnosis was a shock. But when I went to see her in hospital, her first words to me were 'I've had a lovely life.' She then proceeded to live her last months as joyfully as possible, inviting a constant stream of guests into the house. On one occasion, two of her sisters visited, and my sister in law took a beautiful video of the three of them singing songs from school and collapsing in laughter. My twin sister drove her up to the top of the Long Mynd so she could enjoy the views again, on Mother's Day we sat in the garden appreciating the roses her friends had given her, on Easter Sunday despite being very incapacitated, at her own insistence, my brother and sisters managed to get her up and out to church for morning mass. Once she was bedridden, we and guests continued to eat with her, and she joined in the conversation from her bed. We were lucky that our sister Joanna is a nurse, and was able to care for her, and that there are eight of us siblings, so we were all able to rotate the support. In the last week or so before she died, things did become more difficult and as it became clearer she didn't have long left, we slowly began to gather in the house. On her last night, we were woken at 5 a.m., as the hospice nurse thought we were close to the end. But as we sat by her bedside, listening to the rain drumming on the roof, and her rasping breathing, it became clear she was waiting for my brother and sister to come back from Heathrow, where John had just landed. John is a priest so when he arrived at her bedside, he read the above passage, which felt entirely fitting. There was nothing for us to be afraid of, there was nothing for mother to be afraid of. Her family had come from Epsom and Derbyshire, Ascot, and Oxford, Norway, Uganda and South Africa, and were present with her as two hours later she breathed her last breath. For me, it was a moment of both intense pain and exquisite beauty, and I remain grateful that we were able to support her to die in her own bed, in her own home, pain free and so peacefully.

I've witnessed one other death like that, my friend Pip. Pip was a few years older than me. We met when were assistants in Lambeth L'Arche community, when she had just left university and I was about to go. Our friendship flourished in the years that followed as she went into housing, and I into social care. It survived her living in Australia for a year, and me getting married and having three children and less time to spend with her. When she developed breast cancer in 2004, she responded with courage and humour and after living cancer free for five years, we thought she would be fine. But later that year, she discovered her cancer had returned and was terminal. When she had had time to process the news, Pip told me gently and kindly, more concerned for how I felt then for her own wellbeing. She made it clear that she intended to carry on with her life and live it as fully as she ever had. She recognised her illness would restrict her, but she chose to see it as a chronic condition, she didn't want pity, she wasn't a victim, nor did she consider that cancer was something to be fought. So she spent the last year of her life continuing in her practice as a homeopath, taking a pottery class, seeing friends and family, contributing to local voluntary organisations and campaigns and participating in her Quaker meeting. The only thing unusual about her last year was that she knew she was living in the shadow of death, though she didn't realise how quickly it would come. She managed to live in this way until the last three weeks, when the stomach cancer that killed her had spread so she was admitted to her local hospice. I know there were many moments in that last year and in the final few weeks when Pip was in pain and struggling, but nonetheless, she managed to make that time about friendship and love, having a steady stream of visitors to her bed. The last time I visited, two days before her death, she took a lively interest in my recent holiday, and despite being heavily dosed with morphine, and physically incredibly weak, managed to walk a little. The next day, her condition took a turn for the worse and I was invited to join friends at her bedside for evening prayer. As we met in the waiting room, I was reminded of the party we held before she left for Australia, which was the last time I'd met several of the other guests. When we stood round her bed, I felt connected to that occasion, as we were all united in our love for a dear friend who was leaving us for the last time. My last image of Pip is her beaming face, as I leant down and kissed her goodbye. Afterwards, one friend kept vigil by her bed for the night, as she had done, when she accompanied Pip to the gate at the airport back in 1994. She had a mainly peaceful night, and then early in the morning seemed restless. The nurses turned her and shortly after that she died and I'm sure she was at peace when she did so.

## *Questions for reflection*
- Do you believe that God is with you in the water and the fire?
- Have you witnessed someone dying? What was it like?
- If you haven't, are you worried about witnessing someone dying?

## 3 BAD DEATHS

> In the end it was Job who broke the silence and cursed the day of his birth. This is what he said:
>
> 'Perish the day on which I was born
> And the night that told of a boy
>     conceived.
> May that day be darkness, may God on
>     high have no thought for it,
> may no light shine from it.
> May murk and shadow dark as death
>     claim it for their own,
> clouds hang over it, darkness terrify it.
> That night – let obscurity seize on it
> let it not rejoice among the days of the
>     year
> not find its way into the reckoning of
>     the months.
> And may that night be sterile, devoid of
>     any crises of joy!
> Let it be cursed by those who curse
>     certain days
> and are ready to rouse Leviathan.
> Dark be the stars of its morning;
> let it wait for light and have none,
> and never see the opening eyes of dawn,
> since it would not shut on me the doors
>     of the womb
> to hide sorrow from my eyes.'
>
> *Job 3:3-10*

Unfortunately, not everyone dies peacefully. In his moving memoir, Harry's Last Stand, Harry Leslie Smith, who I mentioned earlier, described the trauma of watching his sister die in agony of consumption, because the family was too poor to access drugs.[3] Although modern medicine has moved on from this, there are still times when things go wrong with death. That's why I find the above extract from Job so helpful. It is of course the complete opposite of the Isaiah passage quoted earlier. Rather than hope, Job is consumed by so much pain he wishes he had never been born. How bad must things be if you are ready to curse the day of your birth? That you want to bring darkness, obscure light, even wish God hadn't thought of your birth? It is hopeless and despairing and yet it gets to an essential truth. When things are this bad, when pain is this intense, it feels like God is nowhere, it feels like there will never be light again. So why not make the stars dark, refuse to see the dawn that refused to shut the 'doors of the womb'? There's a visceral honesty here that we should acknowledge and be grateful for, because while we all need hope, pretending that despair and desperation doesn't happen isn't helpful either. Sometimes we need to get right down into that darkness before we can move forward.

My Mum and Pip were both diagnosed with terminal illnesses which enabled them to receive excellent palliative care resulting in the good deaths I described above. Unfortunately this does not always happen in the acute hospital sector for several reasons. One is that there is legal requirement for health care professionals to do their best to save the life of a seriously ill person, unless they have explicitly asked for this not to happen. This means that if someone hasn't given advance instructions, their death might not be managed as well as they or their family members might wish. This was what happened when my father died.

In 1995 he had a stroke that debilitated him. Seven years previously he had had a heart bypass operation and before his stroke the doctors had told him he would need another if he wanted to live longer. He was not keen, he was over seventy, and felt happy with the amount of years he had lived. He had found the earlier operation gruelling and painful and he wasn't sure if he had the strength and energy to go through it again. After his stroke, his speech and knowledge of words was impaired, and he struggled to walk without pain, but he was the happiest I had ever known him and spent those last months appreciating friends and family, and the simplest things in life. The last weekend I spent with him, we walked back from church across the fields and enjoyed the evening sunlight and the sound of the rooks. He looked up at the hills and said, 'I'll probably not go up there again', and while we all joked later, it wasn't as if he did much walking anyway, it was an acknowledgement that he knew he didn't have long left.

The week before he died, he travelled to Liverpool, where he had been born, and took my mother, brother Hugh and his wife Michelle and son George, to visit the house where he was born and his other family homes. He sorted out all his paperwork that week, and the night before he died, had a lovely evening with friends. As Mike and Carolyn left, he turned to Mike and said, 'If this is my last night on earth, I'm glad I spent it with you.' The next morning he had a heart attack and as they were waiting for the ambulance, said to my mother, 'Is this the death rattle?' They both knew this was it, and all my mother wanted to do was to be at his side. But when he arrived at the hospital, he was rushed into resuscitation, and my mother was left outside the door. He died shortly after, without her being there to hold his hand. While the doctors were laudably trying to save his life, there came a point when it was clear that even if he were to survive his quality of life would be significantly reduced, and that it was kinder to let nature take its course. My mother later deeply regretted calling the ambulance, wishing instead she had just let the heart attack take him at home. And after that she was very clear with her own wishes, if such circumstances happened to her, she was very clear she wanted a DNAR (Do Not Attempt Resuscitation) notice.

My father's death was unnecessarily prolonged because the A and E staff wanted to save his life and he had not provided instructions that would have prevented this. Such deaths can be avoided by making it clear in advance what health professionals should do. But many deaths in acute hospitals or care homes are just poorly managed, leading to people dying in unnecessary pain. An Age UK end of life review published in 2013[4] found that people rushed to hospital are often over treated and there was uncertainty about the role of palliative care while people living in care homes often didn't have access to good palliative care or to being treated with dignity and respect. Part of the problem is that many professionals in the community are not trained to give opioids and deal with uncertain prognoses leading to unnecessary admissions into hospital.[5] All of which is undoubtedly made worse by the pressures on the acute hospital sector. Not only that, but as Sarah Malik argues, even palliative care that does better at ensuring a pain free end of life, is not unproblematic. There are more ways than one of dying, and sometimes the pain cannot be controlled so the end is difficult and troubling for all concerned.[6]

When death is this hard, when we see someone we love in that much pain, it is difficult to trust in God or turn to the Bible and yet there are passages that can help. It's important not to gloss over the pain, or difficulty. Not to try and pretend everything is all right. And sometimes having experienced a death that has been poorly managed, it is possible to use that anger and pain to campaign for the kinds of changes, Age Concern and others call for – better trained doctors in acute and community medicine, clearer protocols on admissions to Accident and Emergency[7] and so on.

While we would all hope for a 'good death' like the ones described earlier, there are no guarantees that we'll have that choice. In the next chapter we'll explore the ethics of controlling the end of life, the balance between autonomy and the right to life, all fraught areas of discussion in our modern world.

## *Questions for reflection*
- Have you experienced a bad death? If so, what would have made it better?
- How did it affect your grieving process?
- Do you think the passage from Job is useful in this context? Are there any other Bible passages that have helped you?

## TAKING IT FURTHER
Imagine sometime in the (hopefully distant) future when you are older or have an illness that is terminal. How do you want your final months to be? What will be important to you at time? Write a living will describing what you would wish to happen in the case of an acute hospital admission. As a group discuss your thoughts about the exercise.

## CULTURE

***Dead Good***. Directed by Rehana Rose (2019) In this documentary, the filmmakers follow dying people, their friends and family and undertakers as they prepare for death.

***Harry's Last Stand: How the world my generation has built is falling down and what we can do to save it*** by Harry Leslie Smith (Icon Books, 2014). A powerful account of life and death in the depression.

***This is Going to Hurt: The Secret Life of a Junior Doctor*** by Adam Kay (Picador, 2017). A moving, humorous and often painful account of being a junior doctor, with good and bad experiences of death.

***With the end in Mind: Dying, Death and Wisdom in an Age of Denial*** by Dr Kathryn Mannix (William Collins, 2017). Reflections on the author's experiences of working in palliative care.

***Dying is not as bad as you think.*** A 3-minute BBC Ideas video by palliative care doctor Katherine Mannix on the BBC outlining what happens when people die. https://www.bbc.co.uk/ideas/videos/dying-is-not-as-bad-as-you-think/p062m0xt

## PRAYER
### *A prayer at the time of death*
God of peace,
you offer eternal healing to those who
  believe in you;
you have refreshed your servant N.
with food and drink from heaven:
lead him (her) safely into the kingdom of
  light.
We ask this through Christ our Lord.
Amen.

*Traditional prayer of the Catholic Church at the time of death*

### Notes
1. Meg Hunter-Kilmer, *The Priests who lay down their lives for their daughters* (Aletia website Feb 23 2017) https://aleteia.org/2017/02/23/the-priests-who-lay-their-lives-for-their-daughters/
2. Tayor Hamon, *Online vigil for veteran Harry Leslie Smith as he is admitted to Canadian hospital* (*The National*, 21 November 2018) https://www.thenational.ae/world/europe/online-vigil-for-veteran-harry-leslie-smith-as-he-is-admitted-to-canadian-hospital-1.794311
3. Harry Leslie Smith, *Harry's Last Stand: How the world my generation has built is falling down and what we can do to save it* (Icon Books, 2014).
4. Susan Davidson and Tom Hunter, *End of Life Evidence Review* (Age UK 2013) https://www.ageuk.org.uk/globalassets/age-uk/documents/reports-and-publications/reports-and-briefings/

health--wellbeing/rb_oct13_age_uk_end_of_life_evidence_review.pdf
5. ibid
6. Sarah Malik, *The Inconvenient Truth about Dying* (Medium website, 27 April 2019) https://medium.com/death-dying-and-digital/the-inconvenient-truth-about-dying-1059e6a7665e
7. Susan Davidson and Tom Hunter, *End of Life Evidence Review* (Age UK 2013) https://www.ageuk.org.uk/globalassets/age-uk/documents/reports-and-publications/reports-and-briefings/health--wellbeing/rb_oct13_age_uk_end_of_life_evidence_review.pdf

# 4
# CONTROLLING THE END OF LIFE

**'You shall not murder'**
***Exodus 20:13***

As we've seen in the last chapter, managing the end of life well can make all the difference between a peaceful and a painful death. While we would want to ensure the former for ourselves and for our loved ones it cannot always be guaranteed. What if we were able to control the means of our death, taking drugs that ensured a painless end? This question is not a new one. In Greek and Roman culture, euthanasia – the practice of ending life early to prevent suffering – was considered acceptable. It was only after Christianity was endorsed by Constantine, that Judeo-Christian thinking on the sanctity of life led to euthanasia being forbidden.[1] However, the rise of rationalism in the eighteenth and nineteenth centuries, and developments in medical science, have caused us to question more openly the way we live and die. Today we can resuscitate people who would have died in a previous era, keep people in comas alive for years, have drugs that can end life swiftly. And with these developments come changing social attitudes. Forty years ago, many people in the west were opposed to euthanasia partly due to the influence of religion but also perhaps due to the horrors of the Holocaust. As involvement in organised religion has declined, the impact of World War II has faded and individual rights and freedoms have become increasingly important, attitudes to euthanasia have also changed, including among religious people.[2] This now poses complex questions for Christians. The idea that someone who is dying should take their own life or be supported to end it early goes against our belief that life is sacred. And yet if someone we love were to experience excruciating pain as they were dying, a compassionate response might be to help them end it, particularly if we wanted to give the dying person autonomy for decision making.

## 1 THOU SHALL NOT KILL

> Cain said to his brother Abel, 'Let us go out'; and while they were in the open country, Cain set on his brother and killed him. The LORD asked Cain, 'Where is your brother Abel?' He replied, 'I do not know. Am I my brother's guardian?' The LORD asked, 'What have you done? Your brother's blood is crying out to me from the ground. Now cursed are you from the

> ground that has opened its mouth to receive your brother's blood at your hands. When you till the ground it will no longer give you strength. A homeless wanderer you shall be on the earth. Then Cain said to the LORD, 'My punishment is greater than I can bear. Look, today you have driven me from the face of the earth ... anyone who comes across me will kill me!' The LORD replied, 'Very well, then, anyone who kills Cain will suffer a sevenfold vengeance.' Then the LORD put a mark on Cain, so that no one coming across him would kill him.'
>
> *Genesis 4:8-15*

The story of Cain and Abel is one of the earliest accounts of human interaction in the Bible, coming straight after the expulsion of Adam and Eve from Eden. Sibling rivalry is taken to epic proportions when Cain kills his brother out of jealousy, setting out a key Bible imperative, taking a life is wrong. If Adam and Eve sinned by testing God, and Cain sinned by being resentful of his brother, it is clear here that the even greater sin is Cain committing murder. I don't think it is a coincidence that this incident happens so soon, the writers of Genesis are setting out the moral code for the people to follow – they want to make it clear that taking a life is wrong. The point is hammered home later in Exodus, when Moses receives the Ten Commandments, the sixth of which is 'You shall not murder' (Exodus 20:13), a phrase many of us remember as 'Thou shalt not kill'. This ethic has informed Judeo-Christian thinking for centuries and is why euthanasia has been condemned.

I can find only one example in the Bible where it seems that euthanasia is discussed. In 1 Samuel 31:3-4, Saul is struck down in battle and begs his soldiers to end his life. They refuse and he kills himself. A second version of the story, 2 Samuel, seems to be an even stronger condemnation of 'mercy' killing:

> Then David asked the young man who had brought the news. 'How do you know that Saul and his son Jonathan are dead?' The young man replied, 'I happened to be on Mount Gilboa, and there was Saul, leaning on his spear, with the chariots and the calvary bearing down on him. Glancing behind him and seeing me, he shouted to me. I replied. "Here I am!" He said, "Who are you?" I replied, "I am an Amalekite." Then he said, "Come here and kill me. My head is swimming, although I still have all my strength." So I went over to him and killed him, because I knew that once he had fallen he could not survive. I then took the crown that he had on his head

> and the bracelet on his arm, and have brought them here to my lord.'
>
> Then David took hold of his clothes and tore them, and all the men with him did the same. They mourned and wept and fasted until the evening for Saul and his son Jonathan, for the people of the LORD and for the House of Israel, because they had fallen by the sword.
>
> David said to the young man who had brought the news, 'Where are you from?' He replied, 'I am the son of a resident foreigner, an Amalekite.' David said, 'How was it that you were not afraid to lift your hand to destroy the LORD's anointed?' Then David called one of the young men and said, 'Come here and strike him down.' The man struck him and he died. David said, 'Your blood be on your own head. You convicted yourself out of your own mouth by saying, "I killed the LORD's anointed."'
>
> *2 Samuel 1:6-16*

These two passages are often used by Christians arguing that there is a biblical injunction against euthanasia. I can understand the impulse to cite this story. In both versions, the one where Saul asks for help and it is denied, and the one where the soldier admits to killing him, it is clear that the request is considered to be wrong. However, I am not wholly convinced that it is condemning euthanasia per se. Firstly, the incident takes place at the end of a battle, when Saul has sustained a lethal wound that would probably kill him in a few hours, which is not comparable to someone who is terminally ill or living with a painful illness for a long time. Secondly, in the first version of the story, it doesn't matter that the soldiers don't kill Saul as he is able to kill himself anyway. And in the second version the biggest concern David seems to have is that the soldier (a mercenary Amalekite, who was perhaps seeking reward for his actions), has killed 'the LORD's anointed'. In a time when kings were considered God's representative on earth, it seems to me that David is condemning the act of killing such a man rather than the fact it is an act of euthanasia. As with the Exodus passage quoted above, it seems that there is a certain amount of selectivity about the right to life in this story – it's wrong to kill, but justified to kill the killer? That doesn't seem to be a very consistent ethic.

In fact, 'thou shall not kill' has always been selective in Judeo-Christian culture. The death penalty was legal in most Western countries till the last century, and still is in most US states. While St Augustine's 'Just War' theory allows for the taking of life in conflict, albeit with strict conditions attached. Furthermore, there are many things in the Bible we would not support today, such as the acceptance of slavery, or the subjugation of women. Re-evaluating this commandment in the context of changing social circumstances may now be necessary, but given the complexity of the issues, the debate needs to be conducted in a spirit of compassion and mercy.

## *Questions for reflection*
- Consider the two passages cited above. What do you think they tell us about the taking of a life?
- Can you think of any other Bible passages that discuss life and death in this way? Is there a consistent Biblical ethic about murder?
- Are there any circumstances where killing someone might be justifiable?

## 2 COMPASSION AND MERCY

> 'Come to me, all you who labour and are overburdened and I will give you rest. Take my yoke upon you and learn from me, for I am gentle and humble in heart, and you will find rest for your souls. For my yoke is easy and my burden light.'
>
> *Matthew 11:28-30*

As noted in the previous section, the Bible has very little to say about euthanasia and Jesus himself says nothing on the subject. What we do know however, is that Jesus was compassionate. The above passage gives us an important insight into who Jesus is, someone who recognises our burdens, whatever they are, and can carry them for us. It reminds me a bit of Psalm 23, and the invitation to walk with the Lord, our shepherd, who will calm our fears and take us to the peaceful still waters. Jesus frequently shows compassion; when the people are sick he heals them (Matthew 14:14), when hungry, he expresses concern (Matthew 15:32), and he weeps when he arrives at Lazarus' tomb (John 11:35). There is no doubt that Jesus is loving, that God is loving. So when we discuss euthanasia we need to keep hold of this. Because, as Dr Irene Tuffrey-Wijne, a professor of palliative care for people with learning disabilities, argues, whatever you believe about euthanasia, both sides are acting with compassion.[3]

On the one hand most people would agree that it is awful to see someone we love in intense pain, so that wanting to end their suffering is a good instinct. When Diane Pretty developed Motor Neurone Disease, she feared her life would end with a painful suffocating death. She took a legal case all the way to the European Court of Human Rights to try and change the law so her husband could help her commit suicide. Her case failed and two weeks later, she died in a hospice in the exact manner she feared. After her death, her husband commented that she had to go through death the way she had foreseen and there was nothing he could do about it.[4] Tony

Nicklinson suffered from 'locked in syndrome' a condition that paralyses an individual and their only method of communication is blinking. He argued that his life was unbearable and that he wanted medical help to end it. He too lost his case, and died a week later after refusing food in accordance with an advance directive. While he did choose to end his suffering, there is no doubt that starving to death is a painful way to die, and the fact that he was unable to die in the way he chose was devastating for him.[5] One would have to have a heart of stone not to have sympathy for Diane Pretty, Tony Nicklinson and their families.

On the other hand, Baroness Jane Campbell who has lived with spinal muscular atrophy since she was a child, argues that sick and disabled people are terrified of euthanasia becoming law. She points out that most disabled people and the organisations that support them take a different view to Pretty. They believe law shouldn't be defined by hard cases and if euthanasia were legalised, people would be pressurised into an early death for fear of being a burden on their families instead of fighting for better resources to support them.[6] It's an equally powerful and emotive argument particularly in the United Kingdom since the advent of austerity when sick and disabled people have struggled to have enough support, leading to an increase in suicides among people claiming disability benefits.[7] This fear is also based on knowledge that sick and disabled people were murdered by the Nazi regime under the infamous Aktion T4 programme because they were considered a burden on the state.[8]

So how should Christians think about these issues? When I asked this question of friends on Facebook, I received a variety of responses, reflecting the complexities highlighted above. Wendy, the hospice nurse, feels there is a case for and against assisted dying, but that it is very personal depending on the beliefs, level of pain, acceptance of death:

> Medicine can be great in bringing life to a close if used carefully and appropriately and is well planned and discussed by the medical team and family. But in acute hospital it can be very difficult to make these plans and death and pain and discomfort can be prolonged.

For Patrick Ramsey, a student, it is a matter of autonomy and the role of the state. He suggests:

> Ultimately it's their life and I can't contradict their experience because I'm not living it. Even if I considered it to be immoral from a Christian point of view to choose your time of death, I believe in a secular state.

However, he also notes the worries about vulnerable people being pressurised:

> I don't think that's enough reason to oppose it. I guess it feels easy to draw the line at

no euthanasia because then there's no grey area to worry about, but you're probably allowing for some suffering/unfortunate outcomes whichever side you take.

Elspeth Parris, a political activist with an interest in disability issues, recognises the autonomy argument, but believes that safeguards are vital:

If someone is inevitably going to die fairly soon, from an incurable and painful illness, then why not let them go? ... On the other hand, I don't think it should be used for disability, and the disabled community tend to be very worried about it, remembering the T4 programme.

Baptist minister, the Reverend Dr Simon Woodman, is a member of Dignity in Dying. In an article on their website he argues that it could:

... even be a gift from God to be received with the same gratitude that we receive the other medical miracles that make our lives so much more bearable than those of any generation of humanity before us.

However, he also points out that if implemented, assisted dying would have to be offered alongside excellent palliative care services, as this would ensure people weren't making a choice based on lack of appropriate care.[9]

The heart of this discussion is whether alleviating the suffering of some individuals will unintentionally put others at risk, and whether we consider 'thou shall not kill' an absolute moral imperative or believe there are circumstances when it might be waived. Perhaps the way we have to talk about these issues is to recognise that everyone taking part is burdened, the terminally ill person seeking to end their life, the disabled person fearful that a change in law puts their life and autonomy at risk. And that God will carry these burdens, holding all of them in compassion and love.

> The LORD is kind and full compassion,
> slow to anger, abounding in mercy.
> How good is the LORD to all,
> compassionate to all his creatures.
> *Psalm 145:7-9*

## *Questions for reflection*
- How do you feel about Diane Pretty and Tony Nicklinson? Were the courts right or wrong to deny them the right to die?
- Do you think sick and disabled people are right to fear legalised euthanasia?
- Is it possible to believe 'thou shall not kill' but also support euthanasia?

## 3  THE NEED FOR DISCERNMENT

> My child, if you take my words to heart,
> If you set store by my commandments,
> tuning your ear to wisdom,
> opening your heart to understanding,
> if your plea is for clear perception,
> if you cry out for understanding,
>
> if you seek it as you would silver,
> search for it as you would for buried treasure,
> then you will understand what it is the fear of the LORD,
> and discover the knowledge of God.
> For the LORD gives wisdom,
> from his mouth issue knowledge and understanding.
>
> *Proverbs 2:1-6*

Wrestling with the rights and wrongs of euthanasia is complicated, and can cause painful divisions from each other. Although the Bible may not have the clear answers we need, it can, however, help us to discern a way forward. In order to do that we need to start from a place of humility, listening to God's commandments for us. As well as 'Thou shall not kill', we need to remember 'Love one another as I have loved you'. We should do as the proverb says, tuning our ears 'to wisdom' and open our hearts to 'understanding'. I find this proverb reassuring because God is telling us that if our hearts and minds are right, if we seek out the 'buried treasure' of understanding, the LORD will give us 'wisdom'.

With that in mind, it is helpful perhaps to consider two aspects of the discussion that may help us manage it better. First, when we talk about euthanasia, we tend to use it as a blanket term, when in fact there are several models, some of which are already legal in this country. The BBC website has a very helpful list of these, which I've ordered into a spectrum as some versions may feel more acceptable than others:

1. **Indirect euthanasia:** death occurs unintentionally due to the administration of a drug for pain relief that might hasten the end of life.
2. **Passive euthanasia:** the patient dies due to the withdrawal or withholding of treatment.
3. **Voluntary euthanasia:** a person chooses to end their life.
4. **Active euthanasia (or assisted dying):** someone takes action, such as administering a drug to intentionally cause the patient's death.
5. **Assisted suicide:** someone assists a person to commit suicide who is physically unable to do so.
6. **Involuntary euthanasia:** Somebody ends the person's life because they are too incapacitated to do so themselves.

(Adapted from BBC Website[10])

In the UK, the first two models, indirect and passive euthanasia, have always been available and are considered good practice. The NHS NICE guidance on the end of life, states that the dying patient should have a say about their care in advance, and that if they so wish they could make a decision about withdrawal of treatment (a living will). The kind of treatments you can refuse include antibiotics for infection, ventilation systems, or resuscitation. Advance decisions are legally binding as long as someone has the mental capacity to agree to such actions.[11] This position is supported by the BMA[12] and is a similar approach to that taken by the Catholic Church[13]. In other words, the UK status quo is to accept euthanasia in a limited form. The debate then is less about legalising euthanasia, and more about whether we are willing to extend the limits to accommodate people like Diane Pretty to enable assisted dying or Tony Nicklinson to allow for assisted suicide. And whether in doing so we increase the risk of moving towards involuntary euthanasia.

Secondly, as John Moffatt SJ notes, we can frame the debate differently. As people of faith we can argue that 'Thou shall not kill' is sacrosanct, but recognise secular society might take a different view:

> This general rule is widely accepted and can be argued for without reference to religious texts on the basis of respect for the dignity

of persons, on something like the cross-cultural golden rule, or the stability of the social order. However, the general rule alone is not enough to justify banning access to the forms of euthanasia that many non-religious people (and many religious people too) believe they or those they love have a right to.

While not-killing other people at will is a mutually agreeable social good, not-killing oneself is not so obviously so, particularly for those who found their ethics on prizing reasonable human liberty to pursue happiness and avoid misery (the closest thing to a basis for non-religious ethical consensus). In the case where an individual is suffering extreme pain with no prospect of relief it is reasonable to want to end the misery, and it is prima facie (we'll come back to that in the next bit) reasonable for the secular state to allow a freely choosing individual to do so.

It is then hard to say what further reason a religious person could give that person for staying alive beyond something along the lines of 'your life belongs to God, you have no right to take it, leave it to God'. (This would be better than the alternative (often done) of confusing the right to life with the duty to live). This, however, would not be a reason for someone who had no belief in God to stay alive – and may not even be sufficient for many who do believe in God. Nor would the secular state have any mutually agreeable ethical reason to prefer the position of the religious person to that of the person wanting to end their life. They might, of course (depending on demography and democracy), have political reasons for doing so.

Job endures his misery as an act of faith in the God who will eventually rescue him. It is hard, however, to see the justice in demanding that someone continues to endure misery, with no prospect of its conclusion, who absolutely does not share that faith and the consolation it brings. So the evaluation of the action comes down to personal choices. But that is not personal choice in the sense of 'at whim' or 'anything goes', but reasonable, responsible choice against the background of personal, rational, but mutually incompatible understandings of the meaning and purpose of my life as an individual.

As a religious person, I may disagree with the other person's decision to end their life, I may try and find ways of persuading them not to, but in the end, I have to respect their freedom and their responsible agency.

In other words, as Christians, we may have a moral ethic that ending life prematurely is wrong, but we cannot impose this on others. However, although we might accept this position, Moffatt also warns to beware unintended consequences.

> On the other hand (and this takes up the 'prima facie' earlier), legislation that involves tampering with the edges of an agreed social norm will always have an effect that goes way beyond the cases it initially intends. When legislation changes, licensing something that was previously taboo, even in a restricted form, the ethical views in the population at large will very often shift dramatically as a result. 'So that's ok then'. A widespread change in quasi-instinctual ethical views about ending life, with or without assistance naturally produces a new range of grey areas, at the edge of which are some very red flags.
>
> The existing grey areas in palliative care would be replaced by new grey areas about the depth of consent and the real causes of misery – physical or psychological – or social? For there is a social dimension to all misery and to every death. In cases where there are beneficiaries of an early death what mechanisms do you have for ensuring that relatives haven't been putting 'moral' pressure, creating a social environment in which a decision seems inevitable that in other circumstances would not seem so at all? As the costs of elderly care and care of the long-term sick rise, the state (and its taxpayers) will have an increasing interest in

the numbers 'freely choosing' to end their life earlier than anticipated. It would be easy enough to create a hostile environment in which no one person could be blamed for an upsurge in such decisions.

Then there is the personal ethical dilemma for medical personnel asked to assist. How far are they being asked to violate their quasi-instinctual ethical drive to heal and preserve life? Especially given that what is sanctioned in one state would get them arrested in another.

The experience of The Netherlands shows why this last point is so important. The model practised in this country incorporates both assisted dying and assisted suicide.[14] The decision to end life is based on the individual requesting death because they are experiencing unbearable and hopeless suffering, the doctor providing information, there being no alternatives and another doctor being sought. Since it was introduced in 2002 the conditions allowed have expanded from the person being terminally ill to a number of chronic illnesses and disabilities. This change has caused some previous advocates such as the ethicist Theo Boer, to express concern that perhaps the law has gone too far.[15] Research by Dr Irene Tuffrey-Wijne suggests he might be right. She investigated two cases of euthanasia involving people with disabilities. In one, a learning-disabled woman chose to end her life when she discovered her unbearable tinnitus couldn't be cured. In another, a man with autism who felt intense pain because he couldn't form intimate relationships also chose euthanasia. While the law was followed, and both people made autonomous choices, the question remains, was death the only option, couldn't someone have found a way to make their lives liveable? And had they not had disabilities would the professionals who dealt with them have tried harder to find other solutions?[16]

Given that the euthanasia models of assisted dying and assisted suicide are now legal in many countries in the West, there is a strong possibility that the law will change in the UK one day. While those of us concerned about changing the 'grey areas' will undoubtedly want to resist such changes, the law might pass anyway. Which is where Moffatt's framework is helpful because as he concludes, although we may have differences in where the grey area should be, there are 'strong mutually agreeable grounds for controlling access to euthanasia with enormous care.' Taking this approach means ensuring we recognise the dangers of The Netherlands' approach and model any system on less risky options. For example, in Oregon, assisted dying for mentally competent people with terminal illnesses has been legal since 1997. The scheme has not been expanded and there have been no reported abuses.[17]

Managing changing social attitudes to euthanasia and protecting the vulnerable requires great discernment. If we listen to God's wisdom and work with open hearts, we could ensure that if the law changes, we remain compassionate to the dying, but also protect the most vulnerable by ensuring the strongest safeguards are in place.

## *Questions for reflection*
- How would you feel if assisted dying or assisted suicide were legalised?
- How can we protect the rights of vulnerable people in a state that sponsors assisted dying/suicide?
- Does the extract from Proverbs help you think about these issues? Is there another reading that you find more useful?

## TAKING IT FURTHER
Read the following articles and discuss them as a group. In the light of all the previous discussions do these stories make you think differently about the issues?

### *The poison's still in the fridge but maybe I don't want it after all.*
Paula Cocozza 26 October 2014,<br>The Guardian

When Jo Beecham discovered she was dying of cancer, she decided to buy drugs that would kill her when the time was right. In this article she and her palliative care nurse Annie Lister, discuss their views on assisted suicide.

https://www.theguardian.com/lifeandstyle/2014/oct/26/cancer-assisted-dying-jo-beecham

***Why I helped my daughter die***
    1 February 2010 (BBC Magazine)

Kay Gilderdale cared for her daughter Lynn who had ME for 17 years. When Lynn injected herself with morphine with the intention of ending her life, the drugs did not work and Kay gave her more sedatives to end her life.

http://news.bbc.co.uk/1/hi/magazine/8481751.stm

## CULTURE

*The Diving Bell and the Butterfly* by Jean-Dominique Bauby (Robert Laffont, 1997), film directed by Julian Schnabel, written by Ronald Harwood and starring Mathieu Almaric. The true story of how a stroke left Bauby with locked in syndrome. Learning to communicate through blinking enabled him to write his memoirs which were published ten days before he died of pneumonia.

*Me Before You*, novel by Jojo Moyes (Michael Joseph , 2012), film directed by Thea Braby, starring Emilia Clarke and Sam Claflin. Lou is hired to care for Will who has become a paraplegic following an accident. Will is bitter and angry about his accident and wishes to end his life. The pair fall in love, but can that change Will's mind?

***The Easy Way Out***, Steven Amsterdam (Riverrun, 2016). Set in the near future in a hospital in Australia, a ward is piloting assisted suicide for terminally ill patients. The narrator, Evan, is a nurse tasked with supporting patients to die in a novel the Guardian called 'thoughtful and ethically nuanced'.

***T4***, a novel by Ann Clare Le Zotte (Houghton Mifflin, 2008). Paula Becker, thirteen years old and deaf, lives with her family in a rural German town. As rumours swirl of disabled children quietly disappearing, a priest comes to her family's door with an offer to shield Paula from an uncertain fate.

## PRAYER
Oh Lord, help all who are suffering intolerable pain. Be with them and their families, guide them and bring them comfort. Hold them in the hour of their death. AMEN.

## NOTES
1. Historical Timeline History of Euthanasia and Physician-Assisted Suicide, Pro Con Website https://euthanasia.procon.org/view.timeline.php?timelineID=000022
2. Linda Woodhead, *What People Really Believe About Euthanasia* (Liverpool University Press online, 2014) https://online.liverpool

universitypress.co.uk/doi/abs/10.3828/mb.2014.6?journalCode=mb
3. Professor Irene Tuffrey-Wijne, Euthanasia, Intellectual Disabilities And Autism, Irene Tuffrey-Wijne website, 6 March 2018 http://www.tuffrey-wijne.com/?p=282&fbclid=IwAR1Wrz8uXHFZM2SloHhoVuei7ihJlG7iz4-TwzhDUH_TK9UsEx7qgsBnZ_8
4. Sandra Laville, Diane Pretty dies the way she always feared (*Daily Telegraph*, 13 May 2002) https://www.telegraph.co.uk/news/uknews/1394038/Diane-Pretty-dies-in-the-way-she-always-feared.html
5. James Gallagher, Tony Nicklinson loses High Court right-to-die case (BBC news website 16 August 2012) https://www.bbc.co.uk/news/health-19249680
6. Jane Campbell, Assisted dying: not in our name (Guardian Comment is Free, 7 July 2009) https://www.theguardian.com/commentisfree/2009/jul/07/assisted-dying-disabled-terminally-ill
7. May Bulman and Alinya Polianskaya, Attempted suicides by disability benefit claimants more than double after introduction of fit-to-work assessment (The Independent, 28 December 2017) https://www.independent.co.uk/news/uk/home-news/disability-benefit-claimants-attempted-suicides-fit-to-work-assessment-i-daniel-blake-job-centre-dwp-a8119286.html
8. Michael Berenbaum, T4 Program Nazi Policy, Britannica website https://www.britannica.com/event/T4-Program
9. Rev Dr Simon Woodman, A good assisted

death can be a gift from God, Campaign for Dignity in Dying Website, 18 July 2018 https://www.dignityindying.org.uk/blog-post/a-good-assisted-death-can-be-a-gift-from-god/
10. BBC Website. Ethics Guide. Forms of Euthanasia. Legality of Euthanasia http://www.bbc.co.uk/ethics/euthanasia/overview/forms.shtml
11. NHS website, New guidelines on the end of life published by NICE, 16 December 2015 https://www.nhs.uk/news/medical-practice/new-guidelines-on-end-of-life-care-published-by-nice/
12. BMA Website, Physician assisted dying https://www.bma.org.uk/advice/employment/ethics/ethics-a-to-z/physician-assisted-dying
13. Fr Frank A Pavone, A Catholic view on euthanasia, Catholic News Agency Website https://www.catholicnewsagency.com/resources/life-and-family/euthanasia-and-assisted-suicide/a-catholic-view-on-euthanasia
14. Wikipedia, Euthanasia in the Netherlands https://en.wikipedia.org/wiki/Euthanasia_in_the_Netherlands
15. Christopher de Bellaigue, Death on demand, has euthanasia gone too far?, The Guardian, 18 January 2019 https://www.theguardian.com/news/2019/jan/18/death-on-demand-has-euthanasia-gone-too-far-netherlands-assisted-dying
16. Professor Irene Tuffrey-Wijne, Euthanasia, intellectual disabilities and autism, Irene Tuffrey-Wijne website, 6 March 2018. http://

www.tuffrey-wijne.com/?p=282&fbclid=IwAR1Wrz8uXHFZM2SloHhoVuei7ihJlG7iz4-TwzhDUH_TK9UsEx7qgsBnZ_8

17. Oregon, USA Campaign for Dignity in Dying Website https://www.dignityindying.org.uk/assisted-dying/international-examples/assisted-dying-oregon/

# 5
# LIFE AFTER DEATH

**'The Israelites wept for Moses on the plains of Moab for thirty days.'**
***Deuteronomy 34:8***

Death is in some ways a strange experience for Christians. We are taught that it is not the end, that when we die we will have eternal life that will be richer and more satisfying than our life on earth. Theoretically, we should therefore be happy when someone we love dies, because not only has their suffering come to an end, but they are going to a better place. It never works out like that in practice because we are human – we love our family members and friends; when they die, we cannot help but mourn them. Having rituals for grief are essential to help with that process and learning to live without the person we love in our lives is a necessary part of our experiences. Theoretically, when contemplating our own deaths, we should be happy about what it is to come. But that too is hard, because none of us will know exactly when we're going to die, and what exactly happens next. How our lives will be after we die is a matter of faith, hope and trust.

## 1 THE RITUALS OF MOURNING

> After this, Joseph of Arimathea, who was a disciple of Jesus – though a secret one through fear of the Jews – asked Pilate to let him remove the body of Jesus. Pilate gave permission, so he came and took it away. Nicodemus came as well – the same one who had come to Jesus at night time – and he brought a mixture of myrrh and aloes, weighing about fifty kilograms. They took the body of Jesus and wrapped it in the linen cloths with the spices, according to the Jewish burial custom. In the place where he had been crucified there was a garden, and this garden a new tomb in which no one had yet been laid since it was the day of preparation for the Jews and the tomb was nearby, they laid Jesus there.'
>
> *John 19:38-42*

After someone we love has died, we will all have different reactions, numbness, anger, sadness, relief, disbelief. In the immediate aftermath of the shock of it (and death, it seems to me, is always shocking, even when we were prepared for it), we can find ourselves at a loss for what to do. Which is why the rituals of mourning are so important. The above passage is a case in point. Joseph and Nicodemus must have been devastated after the events of Maundy Thursday and Good Friday. First the man they followed and loved was arrested, then tortured, then publicly executed in a horrifying way. Having invested so much in him (albeit secretly) they must have been reeling with the speed of events. They must have feared for their own safety, and despaired at the loss of their leader and friend. And yet, the first thing they do is to ask Pilate for the body. They take it away and treat it with myrrh and aloes. They wrap him in 'linen cloths with the spices, according to the Jewish burial custom' and lay him in the tomb. They follow an age-old custom with which they are familiar, and it is that familiarity that helps them deal with the harsh reality of Jesus' death, reminding them that burying our dead is part of life.

Rituals are important. Every death we experience has the capacity to shake us to our foundations. Whether parent, child, partner, friend or leader, the person we knew and loved has gone and our lives will never be the same again. Practising funeral rites gives us something to hold onto in the chaos, something that can help us survive our anguish, a reminder that this pain will eventually pass. Such practices can take many forms. For example, in children's hospices, such as the one where Wendy works, the dead child can stay in the butterfly/cold room for several days before being moved to the mortuary. This can allow the whole family to spend time with their child, dressing them in their clothes, having music, stories and music therapy for the child and their siblings and parents.

Hospices are, of course, set up to be places where people can die well and be mourned well. But they are rare in our society. I have often felt we can be too restrained about death when compared to other cultures. In 1990, I experienced several deaths in my personal and professional life. I went to the funerals, some helped, some didn't, but throughout that year, I often struggled to express my emotions. The following year, I saw the pictures of the funeral of the Ayatollah Khomeini. Mourners beat their chests, women wailed and the coffin was attacked for relics.[1] Although the outcome was extremely negative – eight people died in the crush and thousands were injured – there was something about this public and honest expression of grief that is very powerful, and I feel our culture could benefit from being more honest and open about the way we mourn. A similar impulse propelled Erica Buist to visit death festivals around the world to see how other countries deal with grief. Her forthcoming book, *This Party's Dead*[2] provides many examples of positive death rituals, such as this extraordinary event in Tana Toraja in Indonesia.

> In some northern villages of Tana Toraja people exhume their dead, dress them in new clothes, stand them up and even walk them around. That their culture and religion holds that dead people are semi-gods, that they are now who you pray to for good health and fortune, that they're the ones

who punish your wrongdoing. Actually, people mostly just mentioned the corpse thing. What no one mentioned was how visible the love is, how caring the practice is, or how quickly it seems entirely normal to have the dead present. This moment happened after the woman on the left had a FaceTime call to family members who couldn't make it to the festival, who seemed delighted to see their nene (grandmother) again. She's been dead for three years, but she's still part of the community. You know, in our culture, terminal patients often get abandoned by their loved ones, who 'don't know what to say'. They feel like they're already dead. That can't be right. Surely no one would design a death culture in which people have their social death before their physical death. On that front, Ma'nene is the absolute polar opposite of the way we do things. [3]

What shines out from this experience is the lack of fear people feel and the love and reverence with which they honour their dead. And the importance of honouring them while they are dying too. Something we could all learn from. Western Christian funeral rites might not always be that expressive, but nonetheless they fulfil the same purpose. Following a familiar service with the entry of the coffin into church, set prayers, sermon, communion (if appropriate) and farewell, helps ground us, reminds us we've been here before and will be again, that we will get through this. When I was younger, I briefly lived in L'Arche, a community that supports adults with learning disabilities. A few years after I left, Nick, one of the original community members died following a short illness. He spent his last week at home while his friends kept vigil by his bed. I visited one day, joining in night prayers, listening to his hard breathing which others more experienced than I told me was an indication he was close to death. He died peacefully at home surrounded by those he loved the most. The night before he died, we gathered in his house to celebrate his life, sharing memories both funny and sad. When I walked past his open casket the next day, and saw his body dressed in his best suit, it was the first time I had seen a dead body. I realised as I walked past him, that there was nothing to fear, an experience that made it easier for me to sit with my father's dead body a few years later. His funeral was a beautiful celebration of a man who was greatly loved; I was glad to be part of it.

Sadly, not all funerals I've attended have been that positive. When I was younger, I went to a couple of family funerals that were poorly attended, where the priest did not know the person who died. On both occasions, this led to a sense that their lives had little meaning, and though I wasn't particularly close to them, I left the services feeling desolate rather than comforted. The worst funeral I ever attended was for a man with learning disabilities who I had supported when I was working in a day centre. Like many people he wasn't a regular church goer, so the vicar didn't know him at all. And he appeared to have made no attempt to find anything about his life or who he was. Instead he gave a sermon in very flowery language linking every biblical comment about death in way that undermined the meaning and delivered a message that was trite and banal. The only honest moment in the service was when a friend of the dead man shouted his name in distress 'Where's Barry, where's Barry?' and repeatedly swore at the Virgin Mary. Though some might have found that sacrilegious, I felt her anger at God and Mary was more truthful and honouring of Barry than the vicar's vacuous approach.

Luckily, I have been at more positive funerals than negative ones. At my 90-year-old aunt and godmother's service, we remembered a woman who had witnessed the horrors of Kristallnacht, who, in the words of her husband, was a 'mouse' when he went to war, and a 'lion' by the time he returned.

My friend Pip planned every aspect of her funeral. We started at the graveside, with family, friends and children following her wicker coffin, where we read scripture and songs she had chosen, while some of us gave brief speeches about her life. Afterwards we went to her Quaker Meeting for a Quaker silence, where people were moved to speak of her. The perfect honouring of a woman of deep faith who had become a Quaker, while never entirely abandoning her Protestant roots.

Just last week, my husband and I attended the funeral for a dear friend Angela, who chose to be buried in a natural burial ground. After a service in a wooden shelter that spoke eloquently of the life of a kind, generous woman and committed activist, we followed her coffin into the woods, where she was buried under a beautiful tree. The phrase 'earth to earth' never felt more appropriate. On all these occasions, and many others, I have found the individual twist on familiar rites has been an enormously helpful part of saying goodbye

## *Questions for reflection*
- What experience have you had of funerals?
- What makes for a good funeral? What makes for a bad one?
- Have any Bible passages been particularly helpful when planning/attending a funeral?

## 2 LIVING ON AFTER DEATH

> Out of the depths I cry to you, O LORD;
> Lord hear my voice!
> O let your ears be attentive
>  to the sound of my pleading.
>
> If you, O LORD, should mark our faults,
> Lord, who could stand?
> But with you is found forgiveness,
> that you may be revered.

> I wait for the Lord, my soul waits.
> I hope in his word,
> My soul is intent on the Lord.
> more than watchmen for daybreak.
>
> More than watchmen for daybreak,
> let Israel wait for the Lord.
> For with the Lord there is merciful love,
> in him is plentiful redemption.
> It is he who will redeem Israel
> from all its iniquities.
>
> *Psalm 130*

Once the funeral is over, the reality of the person's death really begins to hit, and it can often be an extremely painful time. I have always found Psalm 130 a comforting one in such situations. Although it is from the point of view of the psalmist calling for God to forgive their sins, the beginning line 'out of the depths, I cry to you, O Lord' could also describe the desperation of grief, the intense pain of loss, particularly when it is followed by a request to 'be attentive/to the sound of my pleadings'. The Psalm moves from this despair to the hope that the Lord will 'mark our faults' but find 'forgiveness'. Again, although this could refer to the dying person, it could also speak to the person left behind. Sometimes, death happens before we have time to have worked out all our differences, but the psalmist has confidence that

God will forgive us no matter what. The final two verses end with the comforting image of the soul being 'intent on the Lord'/'more than watchmen for daybreak.' The Lord will provide 'merciful love' and 'plentiful redemption' to all of us living and dying.

And we need to be reminded of that love, because grief is a tough and complicated road to follow. In their 2005 book *On Grief and Grieving*, Elisabeth Kübler-Ross and David Kessler described the five stages of grief – denial, anger, bargaining, depression and acceptance[4] which many have found helpful as a framework for understanding their emotions. Kessler has recently updated this model in a new book, *Finding Meaning* in which he argues that finding meaning beyond these stages of grief is the only way we can find hope and peace.[5]

How we process this experience and go through these stages of grief will depend on the nature of the relationship, the importance of the person in our life and the state of things between us at the end. Frank Cottrell-Boyce's study guide on *Forgiveness*, published as part of this series, frequently highlights how hard it is to forgive someone who has done us great harm.[6] How much harder will it be, if the person dies before you can reconcile? In his book *Waiting for The Last Bus*, Richard Holloway tells the story of a man who made it clear in his will how much he hated his son, leaving anger and rage as his only legacy. How, he asks, can anyone ever recover from that?[7] In a blog for Premier Christian

Radio, one of the staff members tells the true story of an argument between her mother and aunt (her mother's twin sister) which led to conflict through the entire family. When the aunt died suddenly in the street, her mother ran to the hospital, shaking her sister's body begging her to wake as she wailed in her grief. But it was too late. She had missed her opportunity to be at peace with the sister she loved so much. The author concludes that if we are to avoid giving ourselves such pain, we should do everything we can to end conflicts, and not hold on to hurts and disagreements.[8]

But is it possible to reconcile with the dead person even if you can't speak to them? Robert Enright, a psychologist, argues that it is not only possible, but necessary for us to move on. He suggests that we can practice an 'imperfect' forgiveness by restraining desires for revenge, without feeling the need to express love to the person who has died. For example, giving a charitable donation in their name, or conducting a ceremony at their grave, respecting the person but not necessarily loving their sins. In doing so, the bereaved person has a chance to move on and not have a life filled with resentment.[9] Jeanette Winterson's moving autobiography *Why Be Happy When You Could Be Normal?* does exactly that. As she details the painful life she led with her abusive adoptive mother and collusive adoptive father, she also recounts the breakdown that led to some form of acceptance of who they were, and the damage they had also had in their lives. Though her adoptive mother will always remain 'Mrs Winterson', and though she undoubtedly was cruel and vicious, somehow, by writing about those experiences, Winterson is able to find some resolution and peace.[10]

Although I have thankfully never had to deal with that sort of bereavement, I have had friendships that have ended in recrimination and regret on both sides. I have found in those circumstances that meditation on a Biblical passage can be very helpful in setting aside the pain and bitterness I have felt. I once had a work situation that had gone very badly, and I was angry, hurt and resentful. At the time, I was meeting regularly with a spiritual director who advised me to meditate on the story of Lazarus (John 11:1-44). After I read the story a few times, I closed my eyes and imagined myself wrapped in the tomb, bound in tight bandages. I thought of all the things that were making me angry and how they were trapping me. I imagined Jesus calling 'come out', but found the bandages holding me back. Then I began to think of everything that happened, and as I thought about them, I imagined myself taking the bandage off, and leaving the painful memory there in the tomb. In my mind, I stood up, walking towards the light and the voice of Jesus, calling me to be at peace. It was a very powerful meditation, and greatly helped me move on from the bad experiences. Life is always very uncertain, and I am conscious that as I get older, someone close to me could die unexpectedly. Because I'm an imperfect human being, I have conflicts with people I love, and I would hate for something to be unresolved with someone because of death. I try very hard to end arguments, but if I were ever to fail in this, and a friend or family member died before I was able to put it right, I do believe, it is possible to manage a reconciliation after death, and meditations such as the one described above would be a helpful way to manage that.

For relationships that are more joyful and loving, the loss of the person is overwhelming in a different way. While we will always be glad they are not in pain anymore, the fact that they are no longer in our lives takes some adjustment, even if we have been preparing for it. My mother was 83 when she died, after a short unexpected illness. She had had a good life, reached a good age, and was as I mentioned before, very happy in her last weeks. And yet, despite this and the fact I knew it was coming, that her suffering was at an end, her death floored me. Her disease spread rapidly which meant that she went from being fully independent to bed ridden in less than two months. We hardly had time to catch breath with each stage of her illness and then all of a sudden, she was gone.

I had a close and very loving relationship with my mother, as did my siblings. Throughout our lives she was always there for us and as we grew up, left home and raised our own families this never stopped. She seemed to have an endless capacity to be interested in all of us and our doings, her own siblings, nieces, nephews, while maintaining a wide network of friends and being heavily involved in her local community. I don't think I ever took her for granted, but it was only when she had died that I realised how much I relied on her to be in my corner, enthusing over my successes, comforting me in my defeats. Her death hit me hard. I was grateful that her illness was so short, but it left me feeling I had to say goodbye too soon. Living without her unquenchable optimism made the world a much darker place, particularly with the continuation of austerity, Brexit, Trump, work difficulties and my body moving towards the menopause. I'm normally a very hopeful person, but without my mother to help me frame life more positively, I've struggled at times not to give in to despair. Her death also severed the final connection with my father, who died in 1995, leaving me feeling orphaned and alone, even though I was 49, with a loving husband and three children of my own.

It's taken a long time to come to terms with the fact of my mother's death and I've been through the whole Kübler-Ross cycle of grief more than once. At one point, I found myself returning again and again to W H Auden's powerful poem, 'In memory of W B Yeats', a reflection on the impact of the loss of his friend and fellow poet. The poem takes us from the day of his death, an ordinary day where nothing much happens, but which is seismic for both

Yeats whose life ends, and Auden who is left to mourn. It then takes us on a reflection of the world Auden was living in, 1930s Europe full of division and darkness, not unlike today, causing him to question what is the point of poetry anyway. The final stanzas provide an answer that I've always liked but I think took on deeper meaning for me as I mourned – as he sets out the role of the poet, to help us deal with distress, recognise the pain of the world but rejoice in it anyway. And I think that slowly, that's what I have done, celebrating my children's achievements, enjoying my fiftieth birthday party with my twin sister, participating in family weddings and wedding anniversaries, finally getting published, running the London Marathon. All of these things gave me joy particularly thinking how much she and my father would have delighted in it all. In the end, perhaps that is how we assimilate death in life, thinking of the person we've lost and how they'd want us to keep living, reminding us of Psalm 90, that we should, 'exult and rejoice all our days'.

## *Questions for Reflection*
- Have you experienced a period of mourning? What was it like?
- What has helped you in times of mourning? Has anything been unhelpful?
- Are there any Bible passages that have been significant when you have been grieving?

## 3 WHAT HAPPENS NEXT?

> 'We want you to be quite certain, brothers and sisters, about those who have fallen asleep, to make sure that you do not grieve, as others do who have no hope. If we believe that Jesus died and rose again, in the same way God will bring with him those who have fallen asleep in Jesus.'
>
> *1 Thessalonians 4:13-15*

> Look, here God lives among human beings. He will make his home among them: they will be his people and God himself will be with them. He will wipe away tears from their eyes: death shall be no more and crying and pain will be no more.'
>
> *Revelation 21:4*

Perhaps, my faith should have made me more positive about the deaths of the people I love. After all, we are taught to believe they are in a better place when they die and that one day we will join them. But, even if we do believe there is an afterlife, we are still only human; we need to allow ourselves the time to mourn the absence of those we love. This is something Jesus recognised: 'Blessed are those who mourn,' he says in Matthew 5:5, 'for they shall be comforted.' Jesus is compassionate, he gives us permission to take the time to weep for those we have lost. Again, in Thessalonians, Paul provides comfort for the community, reassuring them that the people they mourn have risen from the dead in Christ. The passage continues with a promise that we will all be resurrected and so meet our dead in a future, better life. While the Revelation passage gives us hope for the new heaven and new earth that God will build with and through us. God lives within us and experiences our pain and our griefs, He mourns with us, but also knows the time of mourning will pass. Which is why he will 'wipe away every tear'.

But what does this after life look like? Pre-Enlightenment Christians created an image of certainty of heaven being literally above us, and hell being a place of fire and damnation below. This vision was undoubtedly inspired by the story of Lazarus and Dives. The poor man Lazarus dies at the rich man Dives' gate, unfed and unloved. While he ascends to heaven, Dives dies and goes to hell and is in torment. Lazarus is cared for in the bosom of Abraham and wants to spread that compassion to Dives, but is unable to because of the gulf separating the two. Taken literally, we can understand why the Church preached a message that a good life led to the perfection of heaven and a bad one the horrors of hell. As modern readers we can understand this differently, that this story of heaven and hell is allegorical. We can know objectively that there isn't a physical place called heaven in the skies above us, so Jesus can't have meant that Lazarus went there, and Dives below the earth. We can understand this story as another image of heaven, that it is such a loving place that someone after death can feel compassion for the person excluded from it. And that being excluded from it, is so painful it can be felt physically. There is also a sense in this story that the gulf is not created by God, but by the person who turned away from God and cannot therefore find a way back.

Living in a world where scientific knowledge has ruled out a physical space in the sky means we cannot subscribe to the beliefs of Christians of the past. If heaven isn't above us, where is it? Is it another universe? A different level of consciousness? Does it even exist? These questions are also challenged by the idea that science might also soon enable us to live forever without God's help. While proponents of cryogenics have long believed that preserving their bodies would mean they could be revived in the future, the transhumanism movement is confident that one day we will be able to merge our minds with Artificial Intelligence and leave our bodies behind to be part of the cloud.[11] A theory that raises many questions. Despite the hopes of the scientists who propose it, will it be possible to identify what our consciousness is, and extract it from our bodies? How would our human brains manage to merge with an AI that can assimilate Google without it destroying us? If it does become practically possible, will it result in two-tier humans, with those with money augmenting themselves and those without fading away in their mortal bodies as we do now? Finally, if living forever is reliant on technology, what happens if that technology fails? All in all, while I can see why transhumanism is an exciting area of science to explore, I'm not convinced it will provide us with quite the same promise of eternal life that God does.

So what might that life look like? Some people believe that 'near death experiences' are a proof of heaven. However, scientists argue these experiences of going down a white tunnel and meeting loved ones, are merely hallucinations due to a lack of oxygen in the brain. However, it needn't be so black and white. Michael Chorost suggests that perhaps all moments in time are happening simultaneously so that the person who has a near death experience may be really meeting someone they loved but at their point in time.[12] Don Macgregor, in his thoughtful book *Blue Sky God*, agrees with this, arguing that Jesus calls us to a higher level of consciousness, 'Christ consciousness', which unites us with God eternally, and fits with current thinking about space and time existing all at once.[13] Meanwhile, quantum physicists argue that our consciousness can exist in a quantum universe after we are gone, in other words some form of us could live forever.[14]

Macgregor concludes, the more we follow Jesus' ways, the more we enter into this unity of consciousness so that:

> ... they may be one as we are one, I in them and you in me, that they may be perfected in unity.
>
> *John 17:22-23*

It is this unity of consciousness we need to strive for. And although it is natural for us to fear death, it is the hope of what is beyond it that can sustain us. And if we have the courage to face our fears, we can begin to find ways in which we can prepare ourselves well for our end.

## *Questions for reflection*

- What are your thoughts about near death experiences?
- Does transhumanism worry you?
- Is McGregor's model of Christ consciousness an appealing one?

## TAKING IT FURTHER

Let each member of the group write down their vision of heaven. Come back together and discuss your ideas. Are there any surprises? Any areas of commonality? Is it possible for us to agree on what heaven will be like?

## CULTURE

***Six Feet Under***, TV series created by Alan Ball. This series tells the story of the Fisher family who run a funeral home in LA. Each episode centres round an individual funeral, in a show that is moving, funny and thought provoking.

***Twice the Speed of Dark***, Lulu Allison (Unbound, 2017). After the murder of her daughter Caitlin, Anna is overwhelmed by grief and obsessed by the deaths of strangers. Caitlin's spirit meanwhile is trapped in the universe unable to escape the impact of the violence that killed her.

***The Amber Spyglass*** by Philip Pullman (Scholastic, 2000). The conclusion to Pullman's *Northern Lights* trilogy sees the heroes Lyra and Will travelling to the land of the dead, to release their souls from a despairing bleak existence into the atmosphere.

***Life on Mars/Ashes to Ashes***, a TV series written by Matthew Graham, Tony Jordan and Ashley Pharoah. These two series pose interesting questions about life after death. In the first, detective Sam Tyler is knocked down when pursuing a suspect. When he wakes up, he discovers himself in the 1970s and has to work out has he travelled in time, is he in a coma, or is he dead? *Ashes to Ashes* takes the same premise with a different detective, Alex Drake, who finds herself in the 1980s with similar questions. The third series of Ashes to Ashes brings the stories of both together with a fascinating examination of what might happen in the afterlife.

***Frankisstein*** by Jeanette Winterson (Penguin, 2019). A modern reworking of Frankenstein that explores AI, transhumanism and the making of monsters.

## PRAYER
### *A Prayer for those who are mourning*
> For all those who woke this morning
> to the loneliness of bereavement –
> the empty bed or chair,
> an unaccustomed quietness,
> a life now incomplete –
> may they know your presence
> in the stillness of the day,
> and through the love of friends
> who offer their condolence.
> And in the darker moments
> may they reach out to hold your hand
> and feel the warmth of the One
> who has already passed from death to life
> to welcome others into God's Kingdom.
>
> Reprinted with kind permission of sympathymessage.com (https://www.sympathymessageideas.com/sympathy-prayers/)

## NOTES
1. James Buchan, Ayatollah Khomeini's funeral (New Statesman, 22 March 2009) https://www.newstatesman.com/asia/2009/03/khomeini-

funeral-body-crowd
2. Erica Buist, *This Party's Dead* (London, Unbound forthcoming)
3. Erica Buist, *This Party's Dead* (London, Unbound forthcoming)
4. Elisabeth Kübler-Ross and David Kessler, *On Grief and Grieving: Finding the Meaning of Grief Through the Five Stages of Loss* (Scribner, 2005)
5. David Kessler, *Finding Meaning: The Sixth Stage of Grief* (Scribner, 2019).
6. Frank Cottrell-Boyce, *How The Bible Can Help Us Understand Forgiveness* (Darton, Longman and Todd, 2020).
7. Richard Holloway, *Waiting For The Last Bus: Reflections on Death And Dying* (Edinburgh, Canongate, 2018)
8. Premier staff member, *Is it too late to forgive someone who has died?* (Premier website, 5 July 2017) https://www.premierchristianity.com/Blog/Is-it-too-late-to-forgive-someone-who-has-died
9. Robert Enright, *Can You Forgive A Person Who Has Died? Psychology Today*, 1 November 2018 https://www.psychologytoday.com/gb/1. blog/the-forgiving-life/201811/can-you-forgive-person-who-has-died
10. Jeanette Winterson, *Why Be Happy When You Could Be Normal?* (Vintage, 2012).
11. Robert McKie, 'No death and enhanced life. Is the future transhuman?', *The Observer*, 6 May 2018 https://www.theguardian.com/technology/2018/may/06/no-death-and-an-enhanced-life-is-the-future-transhuman

12. Michael Chorost PhD, *Can Science shed light on 'proof of heaven'? Psychology Today* 20/12/12 https://www.psychologytoday.com/gb/blog/worldwide-mind/201212/can-science-shed-light-proof-heaven
13. Don Macgregor, *Blue Sky God: The Evolution of Science and Christianity* Winchester Circle Books, 2011
14. Sean Martin, *Life after death: soul continues on a quantum level, scientists reveal* https://www.express.co.uk/news/science/1005845/life-after-death-what-happens-when-you-die-soul-quantum

# CONCLUSION

> 'Now the hour has come,
> for the Son of man to be glorified.
> Amen, Amen I say to you,
> unless a wheat grain falls into the
> earth and dies,
> it remains only a single grain;
> but if dies it bears much fruit.
> Anyone who loves life loses it;
> anyone who hates life in this world
> will keep it for eternal life.
> Whoever serves me, must follow me,
> and my servant will be with me
> wherever I am.
> Whoever serves me, my Father will honour.
> Now my soul is troubled.
> What shall I say:
> Father save me from this hour?
> But it is for this very reason
> that I have come to this hour.
> Father, glorify your name!'
> *John 12:23-26*

Jesus speaks the words of the above passage just after he has entered Jerusalem. He knows, though his followers don't, that his death is inevitable, and he is trying to prepare them for it. The image of the grain of wheat is both sad –

because it dies – and hopeful, because in doing so it gives life to so much more. I have always loved this reading because it reminds me that though I will eventually leave this life, I will also, if I have lived well, leave behind a legacy that will enrich others. Whether, the memory of who I was, the children (and hopefully, someday, grandchildren) I brought to the world, the work I have done, the connections I've made. I can hope that these will bear fruit and when the time of mourning has passed, people will see it. This sentiment was perfectly embodied by the Guardian writer Deborah Orr who died just as I was putting the finishing touches to this book. She was popular on Twitter where she had been sharing her thoughts and feelings about her illness and forthcoming death, last night someone shared a recent tweet in which she said she had planted seeds she knew she would never see grow, but in doing so had left a small part of herself in the world.

The reading is also helpful when mourning as it is a reminder that when the time of grief is over, we will remember with greater love. If in the midst of life we are in death, is a reminder of our mortality, its opposite – in the midst of death we are in life – reminds us life has to go on and the way we honour our dead is to keep living in their memories. My sister, Joanna Clark, captures this feeling perfectly in the following poem, written about a walk taken the week after our mother's death.

## Her Dream
### for John Moffatt SJ

i.   *In one of her dreams, our mother bought us here*
*and we two keep returning, my brother and I,*
*her 'pigeon pair'. Across the valley, cloud-scud*
*dim-and-glow washes the scarps of Rhinog Fawr*
*and Fach. A week since her death, the funeral*
*two weeks off and we're back. What else is there*
*to do? Some people think of climbing but*
*can't climb; of those who can, some never have*
*the chance. We face Y Llethr and begin*
*to climb – sun on our backs, pearl and milkwort*
*in prismatic turf. Climbing so hard it hurts,*
*so hard I ask myself, Why? until, that is,*
*I stop, look round at that which no-one else*
*will see. At the summit cairn, my brother waits.*
*I alone have been here before, have dreamt*
*this view – of sharing it with him – but cloud*
*has come down, cold on our shoulders. Silent, we*
*turn slowly in the mist, imagining mountains.*

ii.   *At the hill's saddle, the path I know goes north.*
*It's John who knows the one we need this time*
*and it's wide and clear. Yet I persuade us onto*
*this smaller track which winds below the ridge.*
*It peters out in heather-tangled boulders.*
*We turned off too soon, he says, and shows me on*
*the map – pale green, pine-wood – then points away,*
*way down. And I'm angry – I can't believe we have*
*to lose so much height, only to climb again –*
*but I know he's right, and follow him. And when*
*we meet that lower path, which forks west, rising*

*through pasture, it lifts my heart. John looks happy.*
*Our boots hit bed-rock and – talking, laughing now –*
*we skirt the cliff in its cool shadow till,*
*as we round the headland, sun – white gold over*
*a far-below sea – fills all the space between*
*with light, breaking on rock, on our hands and faces.*
*In one of her dreams, our mother brought us here.*

(First published in *The Rialto* magazine)

I think this poem expresses well the need to keep moving after death. The funeral is two weeks away so 'What else/ is there to do?' but climb a favourite mountain. The climbing is 'so hard, it hurts', at one moment, the poet asks if there is a point to it, the mists come down and the view vanishes, and on the way down they lose their way. All representative of the emotions we feel when we mourn. And by doing so, we make sense of it, as Joanna asks 'Why?' she also realises that no one else can see this view, though the mountains are lost in mist, they can be imagined, and when they finally get on track, light illuminates their path, as they remember 'our mother brought us here'. This is the grain turning to wheat, life continuing, but rooted in the past.

There's also a challenge for us in John 12 – 'anyone who loves loses it', anyone who 'hates life in this world' will have it eternally. I don't think that Jesus literally means we should hate our earthly life, more that we should hold back from the things that distract us from serving him. In other words, when we are our best and

## Conclusion

truest selves, our lives are fullest and we are with God. If we strive to serve God, ensure we ask those we love for forgiveness and forgive in return, and live as God asks us to do, we will find eternal life at the end.

The section ends with Jesus both acknowledging the fear of death, and yet also, knowing that it is his task to die and to glorify God in doing so. No doubt when our time comes, like Jesus we will fear death, but we know that it is the price we pay for being alive. It is our job to make the most of that life, and when we die to recognise this is where our lives have always led. Like Jesus, we will know 'it is for this very reason' that we will 'have come to this hour'. May we have the strength at that moment to recognise it, to welcome it, and in doing so glorify his name.

# ACKNOWLEDGEMENTS

I would like to thank David Moloney, commissioning editor of Darton, Longman and Todd for asking me to edit this series, and to write this book. It has been a pleasure and a privilege to explore this fine new translation of the Jerusalem Bible and to deepen my understanding of the subject matter.

I'd also like to thank Dom Henry Wansbrough OSB for producing such a beautiful and accessible translation. It was an honour to interview you last year and hear your valuable insights on how you went about this vital work. Thanks too to Lisa-Jayne Lewis for driving us there and for a memorable car journey.

I was gratified by all the responses I received on Facebook to my enquiries, and for helpful thoughts from Rev Dr Simon Woodman, Elspeth Parris, Wendy, Catherine, Patrick Ramsey. I'm also grateful to Margaret Wright and to my brother John Moffatt SJ for answering my questions.

Thanks to my sister Joanna Clark for allowing me to use her poem 'Her Dream', which was first published in *The Rialto* in 2019. Huge thanks to Helen Porter and Judy Linard for copy editing and design.

Finally, thanks as ever to Chris and Jonathan for putting up with me vanishing on far too many weekends so I could get this book done.